How to Make Your Husband Your Lover

How to Make
Your Husband Your Lover

LOIS BIRD

Doubleday & Company, Inc., Garden City, New York
1973

ISBN: 0-385-02886-5
Library of Congress Catalog Card Number 73–79645
Copyright © 1973 by Joseph W. Bird Psychotherapy Inc.
All Rights Reserved
Printed in the United States of America
First Edition

Contents

How to Make Your Husband Your Lover

1
On Kissing Toads

Once upon a time a flaxen-haired princess went tripping through the forest in search of wild flowers. (And her parents believed *that?*) All at once she came upon a fat, ugly toad.

"What say, Beautiful Princess?" said the toad.

"I don't talk to talking toads; I don't even believe in them."

"Who does?" croaked the toad. "But you see I'm not really a toad. You may not believe this, but I'm actually a handsome prince under the spell of a wicked witch."

"You're so right," countered the B.P. "I don't believe it. You're a talking toad on an ego trip."

Nevertheless, and to make a long story short, she kissed the toad, whereupon he turned into a handsome prince and they lived happily ever after.

To be honest about it, you can strike the end of the last sentence. It was added for the benefit of any gals who like living in a rosy pink fantasy cottage. The truth of the tale is he still croaked every evening when he came home from work, he sat, eyes blinking, like a toad on a lily pad in front of the eleven o'clock news every night, and on her honeymoon, the panting princess came down with a dreadful case of warts. So much for fairy tales.

Every man must have a bit of the toad in him. And that isn't a put-down of men—or toads. I'm sure every woman is part toad or snake or bat or whatever, but that's another book. Prince Charmings who never croak or growl in the morning, never scatter towels around the bathroom, never come home tired and grumpy, who continually ply a gal with love notes and champagne picnics, shower their women with gallantry and affection, while all the time keeping the dragons and bill collectors at bay, are high on the list of endangered species, just about nowhere to be found.

Our Beautiful Princess may just have brought 90 per cent of her woes on herself. First of all, it might have made good sense to consider something of the background of Prince Charming before climbing into his nuptial bed. I mean, after all, he may have seemed like a pretty groovy guy, but he *was* an ex-toad (and don't write telling me I'm a toad racist), and he had been zapped by a wicked witch. Facing facts, that could give a gal cause to reflect on whether her intended had maybe been traumatized in a way to give him some bad hangups toward women. I'm not saying once a toad always a toad, but she shouldn't expect him to overnight give up his habit of catching flies on his tongue. Then next, just what did she expect to accomplish with that bit of the magic kiss? The story doesn't give it away, but I'll bet I can guess: He was supposed to be so overwhelmed by her big romantic pitch that he would stay enslaved by her charms come hell or hair curlers—no additional effort on her part was required. Well, surprise! She turns into unsexy old Wicked Witch II, and he turns back into a toad. It's as sure as in-laws and income tax—and even less fun.

Ah, but it doesn't have to work out in such a yeeck way. A guy can stay a Prince Charming; he can even develop into a superstar, major-league Prince Charming, second to no prince in the entire kingdom. It all depends on how good B.P. is in her job of toad transformation. We've all heard that old marriage-counselor advice about not trying to change your mate or remake your man. Well, I'm number one in line in the feminine opposition. I like my man to pleasure me, and if pleasuring me means he'll have to change a few things, I'm going to be giving it my best female pitch for change. I too have been told I must accept the person *as he is,* but if the guy is a grade-A slob, why in the name of my sanity should I accept him? No way! If he looks good to me, I'll either change him or pack my pantyhose.

Now, of course, our Beautiful Princess may have tried her best to change her boy once she discovered he still had a lot of toad left in him. But how? Probably by all the worst possible techniques, none of which worked. It's a good bet she pulled out several, if not all of the following: 1. Nagging (always good; his mother probably nagged and it will remind him of home sweet home—and why he couldn't wait to leave it); 2. Tears (really effective; create guilt feelings; also frustrate him when he can't find a way to turn off her faucet—maybe even enough to want to kill); 3. Helpful suggestions (for just about everything; it may make him realize how smart she is, how dumb he is—and how stupid he was for ever getting involved with her); 4. Turning him off when he steps out of line (If he didn't get around to cleaning the garage, she can turn into an ice cube between the sheets; it's elementary reward and punishment; just like conditioning a rat—until the rat escapes the cage); 5. Turning into a female toad (the old tit-for-tat game; guaranteed for no change and no satisfaction—until the divorce); 6. Coaxing (with the right amount of whine in the voice, something may happen; he may develop an ulcer); 7. Screaming at him (He may get a promotion for working late so many nights); 8. Giving him the silent treatment (an ancient female ploy; as welcome as Monday-night football to a lot of husbands—who aren't foolish enough to let on).

What B.P. didn't do (or didn't do enough or skillfully enough) is use that magic power of hers that turned him into Prince Charming in the first place. As a talking toad, you see, he couldn't do a thing to change himself. Wicked Witch had turned him into what he was and he was stuck with it. He could have spent 200 hours on an analyst's couch to find out how the old gal had turned him into what he was, but when he finally hopped off, he'd still be a toad. Only the magic of our heroine could turn the trick. She pressed her warm lips against that cold toad and WHAMO! (Incidentally, do you suppose the Prince Charming appeared wearing no more than he had as a toad? I find myself wondering about such things.) She had some pretty powerful magic, but while I'm not suggesting eager females run around kissing every toad in sight, I'm sure the B.P. didn't have any more going for her than any of the rest of us. And we can use it just as effectively. I think that's the meaning or the moral or the something or other of the fairy tale: In dealing with a man, a woman has an unbeatable magic (or weapon): womanhood.

When we were little girls, we were told all men were interested in one thing. (The older gals never said what it was, but we knew didn't we?—and we had all sorts of fun dreaming about the hows and wheres of it.) It was supposed to be said as a put-down of males—dirty old men, all of them. We were supposed to be little sweet virgin-pures; they were the ones hung up on SEX. When we got all grown up into big girls, the oh-so-liberated members of our sex told us that the other sex viewed us as sex *objects*. And just when we were hoping we would be valued for our ability at crossword puzzles. Damn!

But how true is it? Are males really enmeshed in libidinous preoccupations, dreams of dalliance, and depraved daydreams? You can bet your man's collection of *Playboy* they are. Is that bad? Would any normal gal prefer a eunuch? Would any one of us really want to be treated like a kid sister by a guy who turns us on? Then why don't we accept the fact that men are men—and we women can make great use of that obvious fact? Maybe we're afraid to. Or perhaps (and I think this is closer to the real reason) we don't often enough know how to go about it. That fat toad came right out and told the princess what she could do to turn him into Prince Charming. So it was all easy. What if she hadn't been told, if she had been left to guess? She might still be out there in the forest trying all sorts of things. Or she might have given up on talking toads. That male psychology—and male anatomy—isn't spelled out in the women's magazines, at least not enough to be of much help. But with a knowledge of male psychology and masculine responses, any gal can get her man to give her all the pleasuring she'll ever need in three lifetimes.

That's exactly where the female of the species has the advantage. I don't care how many studies have been published proving that the sexes are equal, I *know* us gals have more moxey when it comes to psyching our mates. We have a special sort of sensitivity which clues us in (if we really want to be *aware*) to where the men in our life may be at any moment—and what they want.

Men have always claimed they can't understand women. I'm willing to go along with that. Even that arch male chauvinist shrink, Freud, after a lifetime of listening to frustrated gals tell all on his couch, gave up in despair, crying something like, "Ach, vemen! Vot eez it dey vant?"

No wonder men don't know who and what we are. We're pretty complex creatures. And, let's face it, most of the time we can't understand ourselves. But we *can* figure out our men, what makes them run, what keeps them pacified and purring, and we can learn to use what we know—to our advantage as well as theirs. If we know our men have some sort of obsession with sex, we don't have to write them off as beasts. We can learn to play on that delightful obsession and develop the same obsession. Whether we were taught it or not, we have the same potential for sexiness as men, and potentially stronger urges. Some men, and a lot of women, may still have the idea that the male of the species wants more and enjoys more in sex than the female, but they'd have to prove it to me—and they haven't. But I will say that sex for a woman is a pretty straightforward, uncomplicated business, despite what the analysts say. We can enjoy love, affection, and sex. Pure sex—with our lovers. For men, however, sex is all tied up with fears for their masculinity, self-image, achievement needs, performance anxieties, conquest, dominance, submission, and who knows what else that lies down deep in that male psyche. Or put another way, we gals can enjoy sex to the fullest without having to lay our egos on the line. Men can't.

So all right, we have an advantage. But what do we do with it? Far too often we blow it. We don't use those two very feminine assets of ours: The ability to psych out the male and the acceptance of our sexuality free of ego trips. But we can learn to use them. And how! And that's what the chapters to follow are all about: *Manipulation.*

Too strong a word? Probably. So I'll come up with another one, or better yet, I'll explain what I mean. There is a lot I want from my man. I'm sure you can say the same. I can try to get what I want by all those bitchy female ploys I listed, but I'll fall flat on my face if I do. If, on the other hand, I pleasure him and that male psychology of his, I can get everything from him I want. I guess that could be called manipulation, and manipulation, as we all know, is a definite no-no these days. Really, however, I don't see why it should be. What's so wrong with getting my needs met by psyching out how to give him what he wants? Masters and Johnson, those wise sex researchers, have a great way of saying the same thing: "Give to get."

Before I go about figuring out what he wants, however, I better be very sure what I want. Sure, I can easily say, "I want *him*," but I don't want him just as a warm body occupying the same street address I call home. I don't want him for a paycheck. I'm too proud, or stubborn, or liberated for that, thank you. And I don't want him for all those other plebeian reasons: security, companionship, a father for my children, or protection against a lonely old age. Those reasons are a little like slip covers on a new couch: They may provide some protection, but they kill off a big chunk of the enjoyment. I want a man who is *my man*, a guy who gets turned on and stays turned on by me. I know that with such a man I'm not going to have to compete with his mother, the television, or the secretarial pool. He'll keep me smug, satisfied, and spoiled rotten. I want a man who'll love me, *love me*, LOVE ME.

Back when we were standing on the brink of our teens, most

of us discovered that boys weren't the mean, nasty, creatures we had known them to be. In fact, they started to look pretty good to us. That awkward-looking boy who sat next to us in seventh grade civics class, the one with the big ears who never combed his hair, all of a sudden had all the charm of an Italian lover (if we knew at the time what that was). But what a miserable frustration! He didn't know girls existed. Or if he did, they came in last in competition with his bicycle, shooting baskets on the playground, and running and sliding (but not dancing) on the gym floor at the school dances. As girls, we were tuned in to the other sex long before they seemed at all aware of us. And when the dating game did begin, it really didn't come off quite the way we had pictured it. Where was all that gallantry and attentiveness we knew about from the movies and TV? Absolutely nowhere. We were lucky if our heroes remembered we were even along. Remember those exciting times when he would run into one of his buddies and the two of them would spend the evening talking about the wrestling team or four-barreled carburetors? And what about the times that one important guy would finally phone after we had been absolutely aching to go out with him and then we would talk for an hour on the phone, and he'd never get around to asking for a date.

It got better as we got older—and as the guys got older. But not much. Somehow the guys never read the same books about dating and romance we did. One thing did change, however. As they got older, they discovered sex, or at least they discovered that as members of the male sex they were expected to be aggressive in the pursuit of the physical joys of the relationship. And aggressive they were. They weren't all ravenous wolves. In fact, most of them were easily put off the first time we said, "Please don't," or asked, in the most naïve feminine voice we could muster, "What are you *doing?*" But nearly every boy felt he had to uphold the masculine code and make some sort of pitch. Was it romantic? Far from it. Generally, it was just a collection of hands here, there, and wherever we couldn't, or didn't want to, ward them off.

It may not have been the afterdeck of a yacht by moonlight with the scent of tropical flowers blowing across the water and the touch of his fingers as he lit our cigarette and poured our champagne, but at some point, the stars were just right in their heavens and we fell in love. Ninety-six times out of a hundred that big fall didn't follow anything resembling the scenario of the movie romance or the short stories in the magazines we used to devour, but there it was. We each found a man, and to each girl that man of hers touched something special. What followed generally made little sense. Every woman has a reservoir of fantasy, hopes, and wishful thinking which permits her to abandon both prior experience and good sense when it comes to looking at the man she loves. Archie Bunker could instantly be transformed into a debonair, sophisticated, continental lover. The guy who has never come up with a date any more exciting than a morning of bird watching could suddenly be changed into the sheik carrying you off on his stallion across the desert sands. Off to the altar and off into the sunset. But then came the harsh realities. How many of us screamed over the transformation in which our men underwent a Jekyll and Hyde and overnight lost all that wonderful masculine charm and gallantry and put on fifteen pounds of boorishness and complacency? Plenty of us. And how did we explain what we found in the husbands who seemed so changed? Well, we might have grabbed on the obvious, "He's changed," without much attempt to explain "why." Or, we might have blamed ourselves for not seeing through to the real man beneath before putting on his ring. We might even have shrugged it off with "that's just the way he is—and the way all men are once they marry and then wish they hadn't."

Our attempts at explanation, however, did nothing to turn our men back into what we dreamed they were and what they seemed to be before the carriage turned back into a pumpkin. Explanations are only explanations. They don't necessarily lead to change. And those explanations that go "that's just the way he is" can lead to a depressing headache. In order to turn the male toad into a Prince Charming and insure that he will stay that way, a gal has to learn a considerable amount about the male sex, and that isn't always so easy. For one thing, men seldom come right out and tell us the things we need to know; they may not be that aware of them themselves, and if they are, they may not want to stick their necks out and let them all hang out. For another thing, we gals have grown up believing all sorts of male myths which get in the way of our really learning what makes our men tick.

But there is also one massive stumbling block in our path: The whole idea of *manipulating* a man bothers us, doesn't it? Of course, we manipulated men like crazy before we married. We thought of it as putting our best foot, or a few other things, forward. Never once did we think of it as manipulation. But what else can we call it? After we picked up the wedding band, however, manipulation, by whatever name, went through some changes—all of them for the worse. We used our sex and all our feminine everything to attract the men who turned us on. We were seductive, coy, flirtatious, hard-to-get, clinging, sympathetic, enthusiastic, passionate, shy, confident, insecure, sultry, bubbling, virtuous, naughty, naïve, or sophisticated. Whatever the man and the occasion demanded, we learned to turn on the role with the flick of our femininity. We learned we could get a rise out of a man—almost any man—with a carefully studied use of what we, as females, have that they want. Of course, the guys were doing their share of manipulating; they thought it was artful seduction. But their efforts, no criticism intended, were awfully obvious. They didn't psych out a girl; they just followed a canned routine. And we knew the routine—by heart. It was as predictable as spring rain. Not that we didn't love it. We ate it up. Provided, of course, that the male in question did nice things to our emotions. But we *worked* at psyching out the men in our lives. I think it may be an ability packaged into our female genes, female intuition, empathy, curiosity of psychology.

So what happened to it after the honeymoon? We found it was a brand-new ball game. Our psyching-out no longer seemed to work as well. And we couldn't manipulate with the same old skill. That's when we began to figure our men changed when they repeated those vows. Maybe they did. But then just maybe we did some changing, and all our marvelous manipulations vanished in the mists of domesticity. It wasn't just that that psyching ability and manipulation didn't continue to develop—and needless to say living with a man calls for a lot more brains than anything we used in those boy-girl dating games—but all the feminine ploys we used so well before marriage were scrapped nine out of every ten days. They didn't seem to work like they used to. We could no longer turn on five minutes of feminine guiles and have him eating out of our hand. His instant-turn-on male response didn't turn on as easily. He began paying more attention to the new model cars than to the fit of our bikinis, and he had his fingers more on the controls of the television set than running them through our hair.

What happens in about 75 per cent of the cases (as established by independent survey—my own) is that there are two parts of successful manipulation of the male, the manipulation to *attract* him, and the manipulation to *turn him into the Prince Charming we want*. While most of us do a pretty effective job of the first part, we run into big problems on the second. Nobody ever taught us the second part. We learned how to catch them, but not how to keep them the lovers we wanted. The man-haters and those witches who set out to trap a man for nothing more than fatherhood and a paycheck conspire to repress that information. They may have lots of fun at their book burnings with this little volume! Pleasuring a man, for whatever purpose, even the satisfactions he gives in return, rubs these harpies the wrong way.

The psychoanalytic crowd have a put-down description of a certain type of woman. They call her a "sex manipulator." And if she spends five years on the couch, they may break her of the dreadful habit. It's ironic in view of their hate thing toward most of what the shrinks say that the womens liberationists scream "Right on!" in opposing sex manipulation. If a gal "uses" her sex to advantage in business, her profession, the meat market, or (heaven forbid!) to get a man, she is denying her "personhood," her value as a human being. Actually what the psychoanalysts are tacking a label on is about 180 degrees away from what we'll be talking about. The sex manipulator they listen to in therapy is a bitchy little adolescent who gets her kicks out of teasing just about every guy she meets with what she begins to think is her irresistible sexiness until she gets the attention and tribute to her power she feeds off. Once she gets a man turned on, she gets her greatest kicks: She turns into a rejecting bitch; she refuses to give him what she has used as bait. We've all watched the type in operation. Such a gal is in her glory if she can get every guy at a cocktail party believing he is the one picked to share her boudoir for the evening if only she can get rid of her husband. If the guy starts talking about leaving his wife, the priesthood, or his favorite hunting dog for her, she has him right where she wants him. She has him hanging at the end of a rope over a high cliff. In one swift slice of the rope, she gets virtuous or fickle and calls the game off. If she is married, she may double her sadistic kicks by letting her husband know about the affair and watching him cry, beg, and bleed before she "comes back to him." With this kind of manipulator, it's all promise but no delivery.

The militant feminists are on a different trip altogether. They don't want to turn on *any* man. Being admired for having what a woman has and having it in the right size and shape is a putdown to them. They want to be "respected" (as victors?), and they're hungup on the idea that no man can respect a woman whom he thinks of taking away for a lusty weekend. They have to be given credit. Except for a handful like Gloria Steinem, most of them succeed. By careful selection of dress (just the thing for a 1932 welfare worker), makeup (oily skin and unplucked eyebrows), and hairstyle (wind-blown toilet brush), they manage to escape being treated as "sex objects." In fact, if they weren't so strident, most men could most happily ignore them. They manage to look like truck drivers in drag. Two things they definitely don't want: They don't want any man panting after their bodies, even if it works to their advantage; and, they are not about to give anything—not even their toenail clippings—to a *man.* ("I hope you realize, Wilma, any aid and comfort to the enemy is an act of high treason!")

The sensible sex manipulator doesn't belong to either of these groups. She isn't a candidate for a head reworking, nor is she swearing "male chauvinist pig" at every man who digs nudie calendars. She uses her sexuality. You're darn right she does. She knows the male psychology, what a man thinks about, what he fantasizes, what looks and feels good to him, and what she can do about it. And more than that, she doesn't have any hangups about meeting those masculine desires of his. She doesn't have to be a genius to know what every smart woman of history from Cleopatra to Sophia Loren has known down to the depths of her womanhood: that a woman, a woman who really gets her kicks being a woman, can get everything her passionate little heart desires from a man if she works through the one thing she always heard all men are interested in.

Before I go any further, however, I want to make one thing clear: I'm not talking simply about the gal who knows a sports book of gymnastics in bed and is always ready and willing with her man. There's more to it than that. The sort of woman I'm talking about knows what she wants in a man—and from a man. She's aware of both her feminine brain and her female biology, and she knows how to get the most mileage out of both. She doesn't think men are all fools. She doesn't believe they're gullible, only susceptible—to a woman, spelled W°O°M°A°N. And in the hands of such a woman, a man (or even a toad) can be molded like clay. And turned into a marble pillar of manhood, a lover guaranteed to be able to satisfy any ten women, and be satisfied by just one: her.

2
Playing Your Red Chips

I want a lot from my man. And why not? He is, hands down, the most important person, thing, or event in my life. He makes my existence worth while. And he makes being a woman the greatest thing in the world. I want *him* and all the fabulous things he can do for me. And that stacks up mighty high.

I know I can get everything I want from him, and then some. Absolutely! I've proved it. What's more, I've seen enough other gals employ the same approach to become convinced *any* woman can get what she desires from her man. The art of manipulation is so much at the core of everything feminine, an intelligent woman can't fail. It is born into us. God knows we all see enough women use it to destroy their men. Some use it to build something beautiful. And their men give them all the rewards any woman could desire. A woman needs only to develop her innate skills. I've tried to explain it in a formula. I call it *Playing Red Chips.*

In poker, as you probably know, the white chips have the lowest value, the red chips the next higher, and the blues the highest. Before a hand is dealt, the players ante an initial bet, usually a few white chips. After they see their cards, they up their bet. Some red chips may be shoved to the center of the table. The object, of course, is to win your opponent's chips, but in order to do so one has to be willing to push some chips out on the table.

When a couple decides to marry it is because each has convinced the other they can meet his needs—emotional, sexual, physical, and intellectual. Each of them has a stack of "chips" to play, and each wants the other one's chips. They each start out anteing up a number of chips, both red and white. The white ones are those things they usually both take for granted. They are the basic responsibilities which must be met if they are to maintain a home together: earning a living, keeping a house, sharing certain chores, etc. The red chips are those bits of bait each holds out to attract the other, and the actions they imply will continue in the years to come. Let's talk about what we women put out there on the table in the way of red chips when we are trying to get our man to make that important commitment and take us to the altar. There are quite a few of them, and we play them all. We dress in clothes calculated to turn him on. We try to make sure he never catches us with wrapped hair or marinated faces. We strain to be oh-so-interested in his interests. We invite him to our apartment for dinner and serve the choicest steaks, the driest martinis, the red wine by candlelight, and wear a dress that shows everything but pure intentions. We come on with everything we have in that female bag of ploys called, "How to Snare a Man." So we snare the guy and what happens? Five will get you a hundred she starts withdrawing the red chips one by one. She now greets him at the door looking as sexy and inviting as a molting ostrich. And when he tries to talk about anything except her domestic drivel, he finds she has regressed to mental age six years. She becomes the total house frump. And all he finds left are a few lousy white chips—and they are smudged and stained.

Now, how to play red chips. First rule: Play the red chips for the long haul, the ultimate goal. It doesn't work if played for an immediate reward. Red chips are played for the *relationship* you want with him, not for any "right now" pay-off. The gal who approaches her life with her man with a "I did this for him, and I didn't get anything in return" is trying to barter. And bartering is not playing red chips. The idea of red chips is pretty much what Masters and Johnson have to say about the remedy for sex problems: Give to get.

The difficulty comes in convincing a frustrated gal that playing red chips will get her what she wants. I've listened to a large covey of females say the same words: "I've knocked myself out giving to him, and I don't get a damn thing in return." They haven't convinced me. It always comes down to the same thing: She plays it "all loving" for a week or two (or less!) then, when he doesn't turn into a lover who pays off like a winning ticket on the Mexican Lottery, she reverts back to her usually bitchy self. Red chips don't work that way. Ever. To play red chips in a way which pays off, you have to be able to forget about immediate return. After all, it's the love relationship that grows and sustains itself which is worth the effort.

I'm not saying you have to wait forever. Red chips, if played intelligently, can pay off in relatively short order. The key lies in doubling your bets. And this is what makes the technique foolproof.

It works like this: You play a red chip. If he ignores it or rejects it, you don't go off in the corner to sulk, nor do you lash out with hostility. We all know how little that gets us what we want. You play more red chips. And if they still don't get a favorable response, you play even more. I recently ran across a man who played some red chips with the skill of a champion. He was married to one of those females who never seems satisfied. Each time he gave her a gift, she managed to find a reason to exchange it. The color wasn't right. Or the style was wrong. Or she thought she could do better with some shopping on her own. The day after Christmas she would hit the stores when they opened. Whatever he gave her would go back. One year he thought he would save her some of the trouble. He gave her a gift certificate. She exploded: "Any wife would be hurt by such an impersonal gift." Finally, he attacked the problem with red chips. He bought her a no-special-occasion gift, a sweater.

Sure enough, she went into her act. "I don't have anything I could wear with green." O.K. He had played his first red chip, the gift. He might then have blown it if he had stomped off in a huff, "No matter what I give her, she's never satisfied. To hell with her." But he didn't. He played another red chip. He replaced the sweater in the box, slipped it under his arm, and headed for the door—cheerfully. "The stores are still open. I can run down and exchange it. I'll be back soon." He returned with *three* sweaters, blue, yellow, and orange. "I took them out on approval, and you can take your pick." Then, before she could answer, he topped it: "If you don't like any of them, or if you think you would like something else, I have tomorrow afternoon off and I can take you down to the stores to shop around." Put yourself in her place. How would you be feeling by that point? I know. Me too. Like a lousy little bitch. You see, if your partner keeps pushing red chips, you have to play red chips in return or feel guilty as hell. If you didn't feel guilty, you would be a psychopath or an infant.

Playing red chips calls for a big chunk of maturity. Freud said maturity is the ability to delay our rewards, which is still about as good a definition as any. In playing red chips, the player is playing for rewards which may be delayed, some for a long time. When he is acting rationally, the human being is goal directed. He is acting in ways which will further the attainment of his goals, both short-range and long-range. When I say I want a lot from my man, I'm talking about *my goals* for today, tomorrow, and whatever future we may have together. He also has *his* goals. I certainly want one of them to be me, and that's where the red chips come in. I have stacks of mail from women saying, with feminist rage, "I wouldn't do all *that* for *any* man!" To which I always ask the same question: "How much do you want him, and what kind of relationship do you want with him?" Everything in life comes with a price. If a gal wants a relationship which is a fabulous, continually exciting, love affair, she will have to play a lot of stacks of red chips. If she is willing to play no more than those *Hausfrau* white chips, she better be willing to get nothing but white chips in return. To the gal who says, "Why *should* I play all those red chips?", I answer, "Enlightened self-interest." If I want him to choose me over another woman. If I want him to want to spend an evening with me rather than with the gang in a cocktail lounge. If I want him to take me off to a secluded spot for the weekend rather than planning a fishing trip with the boys. If I want him to spend an evening with me before the fire, talking of everything and nothing at all rather than staring into a television tube. If I want him to see me as a woman, the woman he desires. And if I want him to pleasure me, sexually, emotionally, and intellectually, day after day. I'll play plenty of red chips. I know what I want. Him. And my red chips have never failed me.

3
He Had to Get the Way He Is Somehow

The business started with Eve, and things have been going downhill ever since. His woman talked him into one bite from an apple, and Zap!, he got it between the eyes. He was tossed off his plush-view lot, had to take a scut job, and ended up with a couple of kids who couldn't seem to get along. What better way to shatter his confidence in women, especially since she was the only one he had run into? And don't you suppose his boys heard the story ten dozen times growing up? "Never trust a woman, son. One bite of her luscious fruit, and you've had it."

As history trudged onward, Eve's suckering Adam with "Come on, honey, just one little bite," began to look like a love gift compared to the antics of some of her sisters. Delilah chopped off Samson's hair. Salome did her one better and opted for the whole head of John the Baptist. Or take Helen of Troy. The minute her husband's back is turned, she runs off with another guy, touches off a war, sits back smug and sexy for ten years while the Greeks and Trojans are killing one another off, then goes back to her husband without receiving as much as a slap in the teeth. Cleopatra, who seemed to just love keeping men and empires hanging by their masculine desires. Marie Antoinette, who was a bit less than being "all heart"; Madame de Pompadour, who led Louis XV around by a ring in his royal nose and managed to get her fingers into what turned into the Seven

Years' War; Elizabeth and Mary of England whose half-sister squabbles landed a lot of guys in the Tower of London (before they lost their heads); Mata Hari, the pin-up girl of World War I; Tokyo Rose, the Lorelei of the South Pacific during World War II, and the 1930s symbol of motherhood, Ma Barker. Does history ever serve up a collection of sex manipulators! The female black widow spider comes in a poor second as a danger to the male when compared to these human females. At least the sexy little spider gives her male a roll in the hay before she does him in and devours him. Some of these gals in history never delivered at all!

A very bright psychiatrist, Wolfgang Lederer, has written a book, *The Fear of Women* (Grune & Stratton, 1968), in which he really tells it like it is. Women give men every reason to suspect them of adding glass to the steak tartare they serve. Then the females heap scorn on their males when the men show the slightest apprehension. Sure men fear women. They've been raised to fear them. I don't care what some defensive feminists may say, Phillip Wylie scored a direct hit when he took a shot at smothering mothers. And even if we have played no part in the emasculating game, we have to cope with what a lot of other females, individually and collectively, have done to our men.

I'm not going to try groping through a lengthy psychology of the male in contemporary society. I don't know that much about it; nobody does. But there are a few pertinent points that affect me—and every other gal interested in men—which require some feminine understanding, and maybe even some feminine soul searching.

First point: A boy has a gun to his head from the time he reaches adolescence. If a race horse breaks a leg, they shoot him. If a boy doesn't make it in everything masculine, he is shot down in a way which makes him wish he could enjoy the fate of the race horse. But the fact is, he can't possibly come out of it all in one secure masculine piece. If he gets top grades in school, his teachers and his mother will toss rose petals in his path, but his buddies will peg him as a square: decidedly non-masculine. Each day in P.E., he showers with the other boys and he worries about whether his proof of manhood is as big as the other guys. The male code says he is supposed to try to score with every girl he dates. But he doesn't know quite how to get started or what to do next. And if he does get lucky and find a willing gal, he isn't sure he can perform up to par.

That old *machismo* gospel is murder. It pushes him to break free of the home and go forth to slay dragons and climb mountains. I think it's some combination of male hormones and locker-room bravado. If he is ever to become a *man*, he must free himself of both parents, and this may be the challenge of a lifetime. Breaking loose from Dad is one thing; cutting the cord to Mom is something else. With his father, he can enter into a sort of young buck *vs.* old buck challenge on any number of levels. Nothing is more satisfying than beating the old man at arm wrestling. And on a more serious level, he can stand toe-to-toe and argue or shout it out. Our society rather expects these father-son confrontations. It's a step toward independence. Ah, but with dear old Mom, he doesn't stand a prayer. She holds all the weapons. He can't shout at her; you don't raise your voice to a lady, especially Mother. She can turn on the tears and melt him into a blob of guilt. She can pout, or climb up on a martyr's stake and have him crawling. If nothing else works for her, she can annihilate him with her smothering and seduction. Short of running off to join the circus at fourteen, and the demise of circuses makes that pretty implausible, there is virtually no way he can free himself of her and become a man on his own. There is no emancipation proclamation for boys.

Since he cannot become a man on his own, and Mother isn't likely to cut him loose (she's getting too many of her needs met through him), how do some men manage to make it, because while they may be in the minority, there are some real genuine men around, actual flesh-and-blood 100 per cent men? The answer, as I'm sure your feminine wits have already told you, is *with the help of another woman*. If the man is yours, then you're the woman to do the job. If you don't, look out! Some other woman may.

At the time he walks into your life and bedroom, you can give odds he has already been burned three times, castrated twice, and rejected fifteen times by women. That may sound like an exaggeration, but I think it comes close to the average, judging from what I've seen and heard in the games between the sexes. And unless he's a widower who had a really great marriage (and divorce doesn't count; it just added another castration), he hasn't become convinced of his manhood yet. Furthermore, it will take a lot to convince him. After all, Mother spent a lot of years telling him how much he needed her and how he would always remain Mother's little boy. He's a walking collection of self-doubts. Insecure? You better believe it!

Whether you call it manipulating, molding, building, supporting, or whatever, the job of turning this boy into a man is strictly the work of a gal who has a keen understanding of the male psyche. Any woman who has lived with a guy for five years and complains that he isn't a man, hasn't been very skilled at her craft—or she hasn't bothered to work at it.

If someone were to take a poll, I think 90 per cent of women could agree on what they want their men to be. (The other 10 per cent are too busy sticking pins in boy dolls to read this book, so I'm safe from hate mail on this score.) The first step in transforming a boy into a man is to spell out to oneself in clear language what we mean by a man. A gal constructs a man building block by building block. It's important, then, to select those building blocks with care so that we know that when they are fit together, the finished product will be that masculine hunk of everything we dreamed of way back when.

Whether you call it guts, balls, or just self-confidence, every gal wants her man to approach the world with a firm belief in himself. If he doesn't see himself as a man, she'll have an increasingly difficult time responding to him as one. Every gal has seen the weakfish males who seem always intimidated by life's little challenges. They bury themselves in some mundane job for which they're overqualified out of fear of demanding an advancement. A waiter could serve them a plate of the week's garbage and they would never send it back. The best that can usually be said of such losers is that they are "nice guys," and that only because they would never risk offending *anyone*. I'm not saying every gal wants a man who will slug that drunk in the bar who makes a wisecrack at his woman. Most of us don't want to be involved in that sort of scene. We do want a man who holds firm beliefs and convictions and feels capable of expressing them, and capable of setting high goals for himself and achieving them.

We also want our men to be aware of us as women—sensual, fully mature, women. Only a neurotic would want her man to treat her as his little girl, or his mother, or as one of his buddies on the handball court. We want our men to turn on to us, to want us, and to pursue us the way they did before they (wel) scored the first time. We want all the romance left in—and then some. Not the canned-routine type like a traditional heart-shaped box of chocolates on Valentine's Day (which we don't dare touch because of calories), but the gesture which says "I have delicious thoughts of you all day."

We want men who will talk to us, not at us or over us. We want our men to share our world and show some interest in those things which are important to us. We want to feel that what we are thinking and experiencing is at least as interesting to our men as a TV rerun and maybe even more so. We want to feel that the men in our lives make their women the most important piece of their lives, and that they feel we have something of real value to contribute—in a conversation as well as in bed.

We want men who are confident of their abilities with women, and who prove it over and over again with their women. No woman feels free to express her own sexuality with a lover who is uncertain in his love advances. We may not want to know where he got the experience, but we want a man who shows confidence in his approach to a woman which says, "I know what

I'm doing when it comes to loving a woman" (even if at first it is all bluff).

And probably number one on our list, we want men who are grown up, fully mature, rational, and responsible *adults.* The gal who wants a little boy for a lover has something going in her head which the majority (like 99 per cent) of us can't understand. If I were asked the most effective way for a guy to turn off a woman, I'd answer, "Stop acting like a responsible adult." Who can stay passionate toward a male who clings to his mother or wants his woman to take over where his mother left off, a guy who can't be depended on to tie his own shoes, the sort who never is far ahead of the collection agencies, can't manage to be anywhere, including home, when he says he will be, and is less help than an adventurous three-year-old when anything needs to be done? Not long ago, I talked with a gal who told me she stayed with the jerk she was living with, "because I just know he would fall apart if I left; he's really so weak and unstable." I'll bet she gets her kicks driving bamboo slivers under her own fingernails in her leisure hours! If any woman reading those words wishes to join her club, return to the bookstore and trade this in for a copy of Dr. Spock's *Baby and Child Care;* you can use it on your partner. The rest of us want men we can rely on. With men like that, women can relax and enjoy the luxury of loving.

If most women can agree this is what we want from our men, we can then go on to ask what men want from themselves. And the answer is pretty obvious, isn't it? Just about every man would like to see himself in just the ways we've been describing. He'd like to feel confident he can meet the world and pin it to the mat two out of three falls, that he can stand up for what he believes in, without being threatened or intimidated, and walk away from the fray with his head up. He wants to spend his nights with a gal who keeps him turned on, a gal who comes across exuding a warm sensuality which says, "I'm your woman, and you do great things to me. You're the world's most exciting, romantic lover. Will I go off with you to the Casbah? My douche bag is packed!"

He wants a woman he can talk with, not just on the mundane level of domestic trivia—the casserole conversations, but on an adult-with-ideas-to-another-adult-with-ideas exchange. He wants to hear about her world, providing she has some thoughts which extend beyond a synopsis of the soap operas or the typing-pool gossip.

High on his list of needs, in fact at the very top, is his need to feel sexually adequate with his woman. It goes even further than feeling "adequate." He wants to believe he can bring even the most desirable and experienced woman to the pinnacle of all sexual fulfillment. He'd like to believe Elizabeth Taylor has never really gotten the "greatest" since she hasn't discovered him in her bed. He'd like to have Masters and Johnson phoning him for advice and Sophia Loren sending him scented notes which begin, "If what other women have told me is true, I'd certainly be grateful if you'd give me a call next time you're in town." Chances are great his sex experience prior to meeting his future wife or mistress didn't amount to much more than a few *in-and-out-it's-over-already* bouts in the back seat of a car or a creaking-bed motel, but he would like to see the world's greatest, most experienced lover when he looks in the mirror each morning.

As for being a responsible, rational, mature human being, well, who wouldn't want to be? We all at least want our friends and lovers to think we are. No matter how many times the guy may foul-up, he probably won't be able to bring himself to admit to irresponsibility. It would sting the ego too much. A man wants to be everything his woman wants him to be. When the bill collectors are snapping at his hip pockets or his loving spouse reminds him (for the fourteenth time) of that household job which she pointed out to him three months before, he's going to feel that old eighty-pound weight on his shoulders and a big minus to his manhood.

We may call what we want from them "manhood." To them,

it comes down to something pretty biological and centered below their belts: *Virility*. A normal, honest-to-god woman wants a man she can love, a man she feels loves her. A man also wants to love and be loved. But there is one big difference, as every gal who has lived with a man knows (but sometimes forgets). A man has an ego larger than life and it's all wrapped up in his sexuality. That stud image is like food and drink to him. He's addicted to it. He soaks it up like a sponge. And any loss of it is enough to drop his ego into a deep hole.

That larger-than-life phallic vanity may not make much sense to us, but I'm not sure living with a guy would be much without it. The women's libbers can claim the whole business is simply a matter of social conditioning, that little boys are taught all this caveman-role routine. Could be, but I still think those roaring male hormones have a big something to do with it. That male ego prods a man to do things which are one step from insanity. Why else would that caveman have gone out after a saber-toothed tiger with nothing more lethal than a rock? My hunch is that if the testosterone level of those cavemen had been about 30 per cent less than it was, we'd be dodging Bengal tigers on our freeways. Maybe we could eliminate wars, auto racing, corporate in-fighting, and the reruns of Tarzan movies if we surgically reduced the level of male hormones in our men. Men also don't go bald and may reduce their chances of heart attacks if they submit to sacrificing their gonads at an early age. But what gal needs the sort of guys who are going to line up for that insurance of lasting hair or long life? And without that monumental gonad-ego, who would ever sail from Spain to the West Indies without knowing the islands were even there and in three oversized canoes? Sure Isabella put up the ships, but notice she didn't risk her welfare or ego by going aboard. She didn't feel *she* had to prove anything. And without that male self-image trip, could we ever find someone to go off into mosquito-infested swamps to dig the Panama Canal or take incredible risks to find a cure for yellow fever? Or get blasted off to the moon? Oh, sure, there are those gals who yearn to climb

into the nose of a rocket and count backward to zero, but I suspect they're the same types who run the Olympic 440—and the
Olympic medics are now checking out those gals to see what
they have going beneath their sweat pants!

I, for one, don't care how much the feminists and some biol-
ogists want to argue over how much is hormones and how
much is "conditioning" or whether it may be all of one or the
other. All I know is men are the way they are (and *I like it—*
don't you?). They have this male-ego-trip thing to live with, and
it has a lot to do with what they want from—and give to—a
woman. And it *is* a sexual thing. Take a look at it:

There are a whole plethora of behaviors which are identified
as "masculine." Physical strength, for a prime example, is a
symbol of masculinity, at least to men. Those old men's magazine advertisements of how the 97-pound weakling can become
a muscled Apollo got to an awful lot of guys. Adolescent males
grew up feeling (unless they were the muscle-bound exceptions) they were doomed to failure in the competition for females. They comprise the majority. The guy who can't match
biceps with the other boys on the block feels he just doesn't
make it.

That's only the beginning, however. There are a lot of other
hangups in that masculine bag of manhood. The Atlas image is
not important in and of itself. Its importance lies in its value as a
symbol of masculinity. In the grand old Jerome Kern and Oscar
Hammerstein II musical *Show Boat,* the female lead, Magnolia,
finally hits the reject button to send her man, Gaylord, heading
for the door. She screams at him, "You're weak! You're weak!"
To Gaylord, that word had one meaning: Impotent. And that
was the *death blow* to his ego. It would do the same to any man.
To our men, strength equals potency. And so do a string of
other things. Granted, the Atlas bit may not mean the same thing
to us gals. Some of us may dig men with broad shoulders, slim
hips, and bunches of muscles. Others of us are turned on by guys
built like Dick Cavett, or Henry VIII, or an unusually frail
jockey. But we better be aware of what it means to most men.

That strength which means so much to them may be spelled out in muscles or power or money or convictions or a few other things. But whatever it is, the pillar of strength is out-and-out *phallic.*

Men have their heads packed full of all sorts of these phallic symbols. Society hasn't brainwashed them; its brain *filled* them with demands they must meet to establish their virility. Earning ability is another. Aristotle Onassis and Howard Hughes are virility figures to a lot of men. The self-made millionaire has that masculine combination: Power/Money. Wilbur, the thirty-seven-year-old clerk in the Water Works, goes to his high school reunion and runs into three old classmates wearing Cardin suits, driving expensive cars, and passing out executive business cards. Whack! He's just lost two inches off his male organ. Money, achievement, position, power, and all the things which go with them bolster that phallic ego. (That expensive, high-powered sports car he dreams of owning is so phallic it should be X rated.)

Of course, the *achievement-power-earning ability-success* ego trip is tied to a few other things, most of them supplied by his woman. Achievement, money, etc., are all relative. One man's shack is another man's palace. One man's wealth is another man's poverty. The environment in which he was raised will play a big part in determining how he sees his relative wealth, success, and achievements. If Daddy was a shipping magnate who piled up millions, success may be hard to achieve if success in his mind means matching Daddy. If he was raised in a mansion, a three-bedroom home in the suburbs may seem one step removed from the slums. But even more powerful than background in influencing how successful he may see himself is the scale his woman uses in measuring him. The gal with a lot of brains going for her can go a long way toward selling her man on the notion that he is a success and that she believes he is. I'm not saying she can wipe out the realities in his life. She is not going to convince Wilbur that he has climbed up that financial ladder as far as that vice president of the big corporation who used to sit next to him in high school algebra. She can at least, however, learn how *not* to emasculate him further by raving about Mr. Vice President's expensive car, tailored suit, and the floor-length mink coat draped over his wife. I remember one gal whose husband worked at a typical middle-income dead-end job with a large corporation. Her choice for a Sunday outing was to talk her man into driving up to an ultraplush community so she could drool over the homes with seventeen bedrooms and swimming pools the size of the Adriatic. Then she'd remind him how embarrassing it was to her to drive down those streets in their "out of place" five-year-old car. I don't know what he had left when he climbed into bed Sunday nights, but ego wasn't a part of it. I happen to believe an intelligent woman can convince her man he can walk on water. Well, maybe not quite. But she can make him believe he has the ability to achieve much more than he thinks he can, and that she knows he's the greatest even if a lot of dumb people out there in the world haven't yet recognized it. If she does her job well, he still may not be able to walk on water, but he stands a good chance of outswimming the rest of the crowd.

No matter how skilled he may be at repairing the washing machine and building shelves in the garage, or how big a yacht he can afford, or how many weights he can lift at the gym, or how aggressive he is in defending his convictions, or how tall, handsome, and broad-shouldered he may be, his phallic ego is never going to get off the ground—at least not high enough to make him the lover we all pant for—unless some bright gal has convinced him of his *superlative sexual talents*. I was recently talking with a group of half a dozen couples about male-female needs. I asked each of the women what they wanted from their men and what one thing they got from their man which was most important to them. They said things like "security" and "respect" and "a knowledge that I'm loved." I made a bet that none of them had named the one thing their men would like to hear. And you know something? I won my bet! There wasn't a guy in the group who didn't secretly hope his woman would say, "That big stiff cock of his."

It comes down to what lays at the bedrock of that male psychology. Perhaps more than all else, a man wants his woman to *need* him. A few decades ago, no sweat. Grandpa *knew* he was needed. He did "man's work," and his woman might have had a rough time making it at all without her man. But today? Well, just how much does a woman need a man? And for what?

The woman of today doesn't need to marry for shelter and subsistence. She can earn her own living, travel by herself to the Bahamas on her vacation, and bear and raise children without "benefit of wedlock." So, while it may be "so good to have a man around the house," the gal of today can live well enough, thank you, on her own.

The whole women's liberation harangue has played this "I get along without you very well" theme in brass, volume up full. Some of the more frightening feminists claim all they want is equality in jobs, pay, admission to dental schools, and the like. O.K.! No argument. But why all the adrenalin poured into integrating male bars, demanding they be addressed as Ms., and organizing consciousness-raising bitch sessions. Some psychiatrist claimed recently that men were showing up with problems of impotency in increasing numbers, and he attributed it to the involvement of their women in the lib movement. Brilliant insight, what? Take a look at the names of a couple of the sisterhood groups and what else would anyone expect: W.I.T.C.H. (Womens International Terrorist Conspiracy from Hell) and SCUM (Society for Cutting Up Men.) Now I ask you, how could any man keep it stiff, in the face of a bed partner who walks into the boudoir carrying a liberation switchblade?

If a man then cannot feel his woman needs him for bed and board and protection against the restless natives, where does it leave him? You guessed it. He has only one thing left, one thing which he hopes (at times with desperation) she genuinely *needs,* something she can't do without and which only he can provide: Sexual Fulfillment, the ecstatic satisfaction she achieves from what he does with that beautiful, big, erect organ of his.

A few decades ago, when a woman needed her man for almost her very survival, and he knew it, her sexual satisfaction seldom concerned him much. He had other affirmations of his manhood, other ways of satisfying his need to be needed. But now, that female orgasm has become the obsessive quest of men, a phenomenon of greater importance perhaps to men than women. Her orgasm has become his last remaining reassurance of manhood. Ask a man to describe his most memorable sex experiences and you find he almost always emphasizes the response of the woman. He'll talk of how she moaned, clawed, virtually tore his clothes off in her eagerness, thrust her pelvis hard against him, and peaked in a score of explosive orgasms. When he knows he has brought her to the summit of physical and emotional pleasure, and he feels every one of her muscles contract as she arches her back to receive his thrust, and he knows that the throbbing contractions of his male organ plunged to the hilt inside her triggers that final female rocket to the stars, then, and perhaps only then, he feels himself all man, the conqueror of Mount Everest, the man who broke the bank at Monte Carlo, the man who singlehandedly defended the fort and drove off the attackers.

And as for her? As she slowly floats down on a sensual cloud, she has just given herself another brand-new day to follow, a day filled with colored balloons and sunbeams of erotic memories. And mixed with it all, she has given herself satisfaction in the knowledge that she has taken one more step toward building and maintaining the man she knows can be everything she needs, everything that is a man. It has been man-pleasuring with a purpose. And what a beautiful pay-off.

4
That Phallic Ego

In some of those ancient civilizations, Greek, Assyrian, or Roman, the anthropologists are always drawing upon to show us something about our basic nature or where we are going if we don't mend our ways, the women latched on to some obsessions which would drive the ladies of the Junior League, not to mention the Germaine Greers and Kate Milletts, into a roaring rage. They worshiped the male sex organ! I don't mean they thought it was pretty great, or desirable, or fun to do things with. They actually made a sort of *idol* out of it!

But that's all out of a strange pagan past. I don't know any housewives who are presently burning votive lights before golden representations of the male genitals. If I did, and I lived next to them, I'd break the lease. No, we don't have any penis idolatry. Today, we can let the psychologists with their motivational research in the pay of the advertising agencies serve us all shapes and sizes of phallic symbols in consumer goods aimed at women. Everything from roll-on deodorants to four-speed gearshifts are designed in the shape of those "personal" vibrators. And don't let the manufacturers tell us it's merely because the shape is "functional." They know what appeals to women; and that's the market. Even if some of it is on an unconscious level, we females have a strong attraction for that part of the male body which is the instrument of so much of our pleasure. So why all the coyness? Why don't we come right out and admit it? Why do so many of us play those dumb little-girl games and pretend we are bored and blasé when our men wear snug double-knit slacks or step from the shower aimed and ready? Just about every survey conducted by a sex researcher has led to the conclusion that looking at the female body turns on men, but not so the reverse. They make it sound like we're disinterested in sex—by nature. Still a hangover from the old "a woman can take it or leave it" myth! Or do you suppose they only survey lesbians?

What he does with that organ of his, and who he does it with, will understandably rank at the top of a loving gal's list of self-interest items. And that's what this whole book is all about: Female Self-Interest. If we do the right things for them, they'll do the right things to us. So let's keep some honesty in the relationship as well as inside our heads and let our men know how very much those fascinating and versatile parts of the male anatomy turn us on. In the chapters to follow, we will be talking about the numerous ways we can enjoy those parts, what we can do to make them feel good, and entice them to make us feel the same, because, let's face it, that's what the real goal is, isn't it?

But first, I think we have to start with some examination of what somebody called the "primary sex organ": the brain. Despite all the junk that has appeared in the pages of some slick magazines since the man-haters mounted their brooms about how men and women differ only in some minor physical ways and not in intelligence, emotions, and ways of thinking, you know and I know there are some mighty big differences. A real man and a genuine woman are different as night and day, the sun and the moon, a penis and a vagina. If they are in the process of evolving into a Unisex, I hope I'm not around when Darwin's law is an accomplished fact. I'm not going to try to discuss all the ways in which *they* differ from *us*. If you've had more than a passing experience living with a man, you know most of it already. Let's just concentrate on how that masculine mind works when it comes to sex.

Contrary to what we were told in our high school days by our mothers and hygiene teachers, men are not always and ever thinking about sex. (Maybe the women who taught that particular myth were merely indulging in wish-fulfillment.) Men almost always have a lot of other things on their mind, things like income taxes, bill paying, ulcer-giving bosses, and receding hairlines. At eighteen, they may have the leisure as well as the drive to wander the high school corridors with a perpetual hard on, but at that age they were too inhibited to do much more with it than Portnoy did. And if the fears didn't get in the way, the inexperience would. A few years and a lot of responsibilities later and no man is walking around like a wound-up sex machine. If anyone is obsessed with daydreams of sex, it isn't a man. But it could be a woman. In fact we know it is, don't we? And it all results from the way they think and react, and the way we do.

I'm sure every man would like to be able to turn on or turn off an erection as easily as flicking a light switch, and most of them would prefer the "on" switch at least three or four hours a day. But no such handy switch is to be found. A man is not a sexual robot, and neither he nor his woman can throw a sex switch for an instant erection. If something or someone is sexually arousing to him, he may get an erection. And notice I said he *may*, not he *will*. But no amount of conscious effort, will power, or fervent prayer will accomplish it. The whole process is a reaction; he can't will it, wish it, or force it. If he is tired or under pressure or fearful, it may not happen no matter how much he may want it to. Or you want it to.

If he doesn't have an erection, he isn't going to derive much sexual satisfaction. He may enjoy some thoughts, sights, and touches, but sex isn't going to provide him with much if he cannot get the desired response from that penis of his. He can even give you satisfaction by other ways and means, but without that erection, about all he'll get is the satisfaction of being a very loving, altruistic guy.

If his erection is important to his woman and even more important to him, it makes sense for her—and that means all of us—to learn how that male psychology and physiology work to trigger that reaction (and what—worse luck—can kill it off).

Some emotional reactions go together like champagne and firelight. Others are just not compatible at all. In a man, fear and sex are like oil and water; they simply don't mix. Sex and aggression, on the other hand, are an almost natural combination in the human male. And lest there be any confusion about it, I am not using the word aggression to mean hostility. I'm talking simply about active, aggressive, go-after-it behavior. There have been more than a few writers (besides the man-haters) who have suggested that every man has a bit of the rapist in him. I think that's a little strong. But I will say that the aggressive impulses surging in the loins of a real man show themselves in the way he pursues his woman, and in the ways he makes love to her. No hesitation, no insecurity, and no temerity trips him up and leaves her waiting and wondering. He's sure of his goal and he goes after it.

As he sails his ship full steam toward port, however, she can fire a torpedo and hit him right below the water line. His sexual aggression—and phallic ego—can't survive an assault of female hostility, rejection, or bitchiness. It can't even survive a fear of same. It doesn't make any difference where the fear comes from. If a man experiences it strongly, he can wave good-by to his erection—or just never get one to begin with. And there's another thing which is interesting in the matter of compatible and incompatible responses: A woman can experience fear and still be sexually aroused (within limits, of course; I can't imagine enjoying sex while going over Niagara Falls in a barrel, regardless of the wild movements it might provide). A degree of fear may even add to her sexy feelings. The gal who puts off the husband with that "I'm just too scared of it all" routine had better hope her man never finds out the truth. Remember those days in parked cars? A stray cat would run through the bushes or a passing car would flash it's lights and he'd jump like his mother just stuck a flashlight in the window. But our reaction was usually, "Oh, come on, honey, it was nothing; we don't have to stop." And despite all those horror tales we heard about that sacrificial bloodletting called "defloration," we still went after it wet and panting. No man could attain even the beginnings of an erect organ under similar circumstances (as every gal who has gotten too vigorously playful in where she bites has discovered). The response which is incompatible with erotic feelings for a woman is, you guessed it, aggression. And I sure don't mean a gal can't initiate sex or take on the "aggressive" role in their love-making, but those are delightful male-female games. If she ever becomes *genuinely* aggressive in her approach, she may not only turn off every male but the masochists, she will flip herself into frigidity.

The reason fear or anxiety or even hostility turns off his erection (and also often causes him to have premature ejaculation) has something to do with his autonomic nervous system, but we don't have to become brain surgeons to know what happens in the pathways between his cranium and his crotch. It's simple. The more relaxed he is, the more he is free from tension, and the more he has his life all together, the lustier will his life be. (You see, a bitchy unsexed female could use the information in reverse. Turn him into an anxiety neurotic and there will be only one part sure not to be tense when he climbs into bed. Can any woman be that crazy?)

So good old feminine self-interest says keep his world tranquil and loose. But how? I live with a man who always has fifteen different projects going at once. He needs five hands just to handle the phones and a smart tax lawyer to keep him from developing ulcers. Telling him to relax and become a happy mushroom would make as much sense as telling the Sphinx to become the Bolshoi Ballet. And I'm not sure I'd want to even if it worked. Sure, I'd like to be able to work some magic and turn off the demands of his world and the drive which keeps him going at twice the speed of sound, but he's the man I wanted, the man I still want, and that drive of his had a lot to do with it.

I could never be turned-on by a satisfied clod. When he walks in that door and that phone gets shut off, that's where I come in. On the Grand Banks, the women watch their men go to sea. After fighting the freezing cold and the angry waves on their tiny boats, the men come home to their safe harbor. And there, waiting to offer the warmth and comfort of their own snug harbor are the women. When her man walks through her door after a day of battling the storms, the intelligent self-interested gal welcomes him to a haven of tranquillity. She knows what every smart woman knows: that only if his anxiety level is low and his tensions eased will he be erotically responsive to her and the skilled lover she wants. But let's face facts: If that's what every smart woman knows, the average intelligence for our sex can't be very high. We do such dumb things! The guy walks in the door with his blood pressure into orbit and that "I'm beat down to my shoe tops and in desperate need of a drink" expression. So what do we dumb-dumbs do? We lay all our problems on him before he can uncork the scotch. And we keep up the marathon of domestic misery through dinner and on to the late news on the tube. Then we wonder what happened to that romantic lover we once knew. We shouldn't. It's a simple matter of the way the lower part of his body is hooked up to his brain, and if anyone has the finger on the switch, it is his woman.

So should the gal, who wants to keep her man tranquil and turned-on, keep him wrapped in a protective blanket against the realities of the world? Must we build a psychological moat around our men if we hope to keep them from the wipe-out of impotence? Forget it! If a man is that fragile, who wants him? Not me. Or you? But we still can't change that old physical law which says he can't be expected to get it up if his anxiety (or hostility) is considerably higher than his passion. So it does make sense, doesn't it, to give self-interest some thought to when and where we lay all that gloom on our men? Let's face it, we can handle most of the day-by-day hassle without all that "tell and share." And we don't need to make a pitch for sympathy. As for me, I'd much rather keep his home port one of calm waters. If I do have to bring him something less than goodies in the news of the day, I try to get it all together in one short period, get it over with, and then go back to being strictly lovers. And seven out of ten times, it works.

Thanks to a lot of poisonous propaganda about the difference in the sexes, just about every man who has ever climbed in bed with a woman suffers, or has suffered at some point in his life, from anxiety over what he can or cannot do with that penis of his and how his woman may or may not respond to it. If she acts like that male organ of his leaves her slightly bored, she might as well pack her bags and get out before he does. He has been brainwashed all his life into believing that penises should always be hidden by fig leaves. The brainwashing has been so effective that it was a man, one of the popes, who started that disappointing business of cementing fig leaves on statues. You can bet he didn't take a vote of women before he did it! Today, my man can pick up a collection of magazines almost anywhere which photographically present the female of the species in all her pubic-haired glory, but where do we find magazines for women which picture a rugged-looking guy stepping from the shower with an erection? We can't even find pictures of maleness in a less obvious state. What kind of inference can a man—or a woman—draw from that? Right. That a woman in all her naked glory is beautiful but a man in the same state is repulsive or obscene. It seems some women and a lot of men have accepted the notion. Sad to say, a lot of guys expect their women to be turned off by what they expose when they drop their shorts. It sometimes takes a lot of persuasion by way of words and actions for a smart gal to convince her man otherwise.

This is partially perhaps owing to the fact that a woman in the nude is never as exposed as a man in the nude. In a way, she can never be totally naked. Her genitals are really "private parts." Even if she shaves her pubic area as bare as a five-year-old, she can walk around all day at a nudist camp without revealing what she has between her thighs. Some husbands have sex with their wives for years without ever seeing what her gynecologist sees on the first office visit. But whatever a man has, he shows. A gal could sit in the fortieth row at a bullfight and write a consumer report on the sexual anatomy of each matador dressed in those skin-tight "suits of lights." A gal can wear hot pants which look like they're painted on her and be randy enough to want to tear the clothes off her man without anyone knowing it. But if he steps from the shower filled with ideas, no towel around the waist is going to hide it from her. He reveals his thoughts as well as his anatomy. And he's vulnerable. If she lets him know she finds it boring or annoying or simply impolite to point, she may find him in a similar state less and less in the future—or at least *her* future.

Suppose that man of yours never complimented you on your hairstyle, your figure, or the way you dress for him. (And let's assume we give our men something to compliment us on.) How would you feel? You know and so do I. God knows we've both heard enough women complain of it. Yet, you know, I've talked to scores of women who never once complimented their men on the beauty of that masculine organ. Maybe it's because we females are raised to expect the compliments but not to give them. Certainly every woman with a healthy love life knows how much pleasure she owes to that gorgeous penis. And if she's honest, she will admit how much she enjoys looking at it, touching it, and doing a lot of other things with it. So I say let's change this feminine "take but don't give" approach. It's fun watching him step from his shower, limp, swinging gently from side to side. And when his balls hang down, loose, one slightly lower than the other. And what gal doesn't get turned on watching it lengthen and become erect, knowing she is the one responsible? Or feeling it stiffen in your hand? When he's fully aroused and you see that drop or two of clear fluid appear on the head of it, doesn't it send great feelings all through you? Of course it does. Tell him in words as well as actions all those things you like about it. Sure he may already know it by your actions, but that's no reason not to tell him. His actions tell you he loves you, but you never tire of hearing the words, do you?

In following chapters we'll get down to the delightful business of what can be done to make that penis of his feel best, but first, there are a few more things which need to be said about his phallic ego and how you respond to him. Just about every teenage boy has suffered with the fear that his girlfriend might have discerned that erection he had on the dance floor. (Of course we did, and it gave us nice feelings, but we never let on.) But with his mistress, a man often has somewhat the opposite anxiety. Her behavior lets him know she is in a loving mood, but now with the two of them nude in the shower or in bed or elsewhere together, he doesn't have an erection. He then may start worrying either about her reaction then and there or about whether he will be able to achieve the erection she seems to expect and desire. And as we know, anxiety is the enemy of erection. It may be due to the male obsession with penis size. I don't know. Of course his penis is smaller when limp. (It doesn't have much relation to erection size.) Perhaps some men feel kind of embarrassed standing or lying there with a limp penis when they know what the gal has in mind. The guy may fear she will feel rejected—or even insulted—if he doesn't stand at attention when she turns on the warmth. That, of course, is the last thing in the world you would want him to feel concern over. And if you play your feminine cards right, he never will. Remember, first of all, that his erection is a *reaction*. It isn't something he can turn on when he feels like it or you feel like it. The two of you will get a rise out of that penis when the sexual vibes are right for him. And they won't be right if he feels sheepish about its downcast state of flaccidity. Let him know how much you enjoy looking at it and playing with it those times when it isn't standing up all eager and impatient. And it is fun, isn't it? It has such a different feel. There are times I wish I could play with it that way just a little longer, but it can't be ordered to stay soft any more than it can be commanded to stiffen. Incidentally, if you want him to get an erection in a hurry, you might try telling him to keep it soft. The more he thinks about *that*, the quicker he will be "defeated" by a stiff, upright proof of his masculinity. If you begin fondling him before he has an erection, don't go after it as if he has switches you can throw to get the response. If you grip his penis and begin furiously pulling on it in that up and down masturbatory way, he will probably interpret it as a demand. And that, as you and I know, is the kiss of death to the loving. If you're going to fondle him (and if he doesn't show that he likes it, for the sake of common sense, lay off!), do it in a way that shows him you enjoy the sight and touch of him the way he is—whether he responds with an erection or not. Make sure you let him know there are times when you enjoy looking at him, touching him, even kissing him there when a full session of lovemaking isn't expected. Then if it does happen, great! If it doesn't, you've still had a beautiful time of it.

5

A Lady's Education in Dirty Books

Every girl interested in men should take a course in the literature of contemporary hard-core pornography. I don't mean the
psychological meanderings of *Portnoy's Complaint* or the underground Victorian novels such as *Lady Chatterley's Lover* or
Fanny Hill. She should get a good exposure to the modern-day
lusty novel. As a college course, it could be titled something like
A Survey of Twentieth-Century Smut. But with the state our
colleges are in, a state of programmed irrelevancy, we don't
stand a chance of finding such a course. Not even Vassar and
Bryn Mawr offer anything in horny books (and they need it
the most!).

According to most authorities who have written on the subject,
most pornography is written *by* men *for* men. (Personally, I
think some of it is written by gals who have a keen knowledge
of male psychology, whatever pen name they use.) If it is true
that men are the biggest market for the hard-core sex novels,
then the dirty-book writer, if he or she is to be successful, must
know more than a little of the fantasies which will turn on a
man. After all, if I write a cookbook filled with nothing but
recipes for stewed toads and the like, who will buy it? So if
men are writing the porno novels, and these men are tuned in
to what their male readers will respond to, then doesn't it stand

to reason we gals might be able to pick up some valuable information by studying the same source material?

Of course, I'm sure there may be some who will suspect me of encouraging women to read racy material for the erotic feelings it may stimulate. Well, just between the two of us, I can't think of many better reasons. But the other reason has something more to do with our female designs on men. The more we learn about what goes on in the secret sexual recesses of their minds, the more we can score successes in our pleasuring techniques. In a word, we can learn how to feed their fantasies and turn some of them into reality. So apart from the fact that a sex novel makes more fun reading than the things we used to write book reports on in literature classes, there is good reason for completing some homework in eroticism.

For any gal who might think otherwise, let me quickly point out that most hard-core books today try to corner the entire male market by offering a little something for everyone. The authors try to throw in at least one scene portraying every conceivable sexual variation. There will be something for the sadomasochists, a chapter for the guys who dream of fourteen-year-old Lolitas, and maybe even an incest sequence.

I'm not suggesting that all men are harboring surging urges for every kinky sex act recorded by Freud and Krafft-Ebing. I know my man isn't, although he is a great believer in the benefits of variety, and I'm all for that. Men are not any kookier than women when it comes to sex. Fortunately, most of us are not sleeping with sex psychos. Anyway, I'll have something to say about kinky sex, what it is and is not and what, if anything, to do about it, later on. The weird stuff in the porno novel is, however, usually incidental. It's the basic male fantasies we are interested in.

As we browse our typical porno novel, one of the first things which strikes us is the characterization of the "hero." He is truly incredible, the ultimate male chauvinist, a true "love 'em and leave 'em" bull in a pasture of heifers in heat. He refuses to be ensnared by *any* female. Leaping from bed to bed like a superman with satyriasis, he leaves a trail of gals glassy-eyed and satiated, but he never succumbs to the lures of any. How this Agent 007 type manages to get every one of these conquests coming back time after time clawing at his slacks is understandable only if we can assume the members of our sex get their greatest kicks being tossed out of bed two minutes after the hero reaches his climax. But we don't have to worry about that. We're talking about male fantasies, and fantasies can always be exaggerations of reality, even out-and-out distortions. Isn't that what they're supposed to be?

If the writer is successful, the male reader can fantasy himself as the "hero" of the novel. He can vicariously enjoy the thrill of the conquest, the satisfaction in subduing the virgin, the nun, or the haughty duchess. With the power of his virility and sexual prowess, he can tame the most arrogant shrew. It's part of what every man would like to believe: that given a wild roll in the hay, any woman can be turned into a complacent, purring pussycat. (I know at this point the feminist code says I'm supposed to refute that idea and say, "A woman needs more than that; she needs to be accepted as an equal, and respected for her mind, etc., etc., etc., but I'm pledged to honesty, and the facts are: Most of us *will* lap a saucer of milk and purr like crazy if we latch on to a real loving man.) The deep down desire of every man is to prove his PENIS POWER!

There is an aggressiveness in this which borders on hostility. But it doesn't mean the average man holds a hatred for women. Quite a few of them might have reason to store a few resentments, but they aren't trying to keep up a pitched battle of the sexes. They want to be lovers, not fighters. There is the element of the conquest, however, which both sexes need to understand. When a man and women engage in sex, they most frequently play out a mock battle in which the invader (the man) conquers the defender (the woman) until at last the defender surrenders to the superior force of the invader. He pursues and "takes" her, and no matter how much she may want to resist, she finally finds his virility irresistible; she virtually begs to be "subjected" by his "penis power." In one slightly overdrawn example of this phallic Genghis Khan fantasy, the armies of some Roman emperor take captive a number of beautiful young virgins. (The ugly ones, I guess, they sent home, and the non-virgins got off scot free.) Then, for the entertainment of the aristocratic swingers of Rome, a show is put on in the Coliseum. A well-endowed, appropriately frightened virgin is turned loose in the arena followed by a sexually deprived male nubian slave who goes for her like a starving man after a chunk of rare roast beef. But this sex-starved stud isn't some sort of run-of-the-mill rapist. Before he takes her maidenhead, he gives her just about every wild sort of erotic pleasuring conceivable. When he finally gets to it, the little virgin is not only eager to be "raped," she taunts him when he can't go on after the fourth or fifth time.

The male conquest fantasy has its parallel in our sex. One of the common fantasies among gals is the rape fantasy. I don't think one gal in ten thousand actually wants to be raped. Furthermore, only a few psychopaths among the male population are prowling the streets with rape in mind. But a whole lot of gals get warm feelings deep inside daydreaming about having their clothes ripped off and their bodies "ravished" (pleasurably, of course) by some great big hunk of lusty masculinity. It sure is nice if we can enjoy fantasies compatible with those of our men, and frequently we do, if we can bring ourselves to admit it. There is one thing which gets in the way: Men have been led to believe so damned much nonsense about us. Sexologists with more words than knowledge have written about our sex in a way that makes us all look like timid and lightly frigid little girls who must be handled with utmost gentleness; we do get offended and shook so easily, and our thoughts of sex, if we ever have any, are something out of organdy, lace, and gardenia corsages for the high school prom. I don't have any estimate of how many gals I have talked with who would love nothing better than to have their man carry them off to the bedroom—or someplace even more exciting—and tear the bikini panties off them. But they never let *him* know it. Pity! Through the porno novel, he can live it out vicariously.

The next feature which runs through the tale is a male stamina which is, for want of a better word, *unbelievable*. I remember one erotic fiction piece in which the wandering lover bestows his sexual favors in an incredible number of ways on a pair of teen-age sisters several times each during the course of a late evening, then does the same for an insatiable maid in the household. In the early morning hours, he does the same for the girl's mother while the girls and the maid sleep off their sexual exhaustion (but not the hero; he's still bright-eyed and predatory). Finally, he showers and is off to an early morning business appointment—and seduces a gal he meets on the commuter train, sending her into multiple orgasms in a standing position in the vestibule of a careening railway car. ("The speeding train whipped us from side to side. The vibrations as the wheels moved across the rail spaces sent paroxysms of ecstasy through her body and I actually feared she might faint as she moaned in climax after climax.") If the reader kept score, I'm sure he would have to agree the fictional hero won the ball game, whatever the game was: Eleven times, all the way, with five different gals, over an eight-hour period. And the following night he equalled the record!

Now this is a theme of porno novels I have never understood. I can see why a man might dream of being able to go a score of times in a single night. It would give that phallic ego a mighty boost. But reading about such a sexual superman, even if he is created out of some novelist's imagination, would seem to me to lead to some nagging feelings of inadequacy in the male reader whose record is two or three times over a twenty-four-hour stay in a motel on his honeymoon. If it does give rise to such feelings, however, it doesn't stop the writers from providing such portrayals or the male readers from buying their paperbacks. As their women, all we need to know is that the perpetual-sex-machine male is part of the masculine fantasy. It's information we can put to good use.

One thing you'll find in every one of these novels is a physical description of the man which includes a huge penis. The size of the hero's penis is supposed to be what thrills the women when they see it and leaves them limp and satiated when they experience what he does with it. It makes no difference that less than one woman in maybe a hundred is in search of the longest male organ in town, or that most men are built about the same, or that a woman can accommodate and be sexually satisfied by whatever her man has to offer in size. Men have this persistent hangup over size. They associate it with masculinity, and they are convinced a woman's love life is measured in phallic inches. And furthermore, from what I've heard, only about one man in ten thinks his pride and joy is a big as the other guy's. The fact that we gals may not see it as a "crucial issue" doesn't mean we can afford to shrug it off. It is far too important to the phallic ego.

There are a few other features found in the average hard-core erotic story which may give us some insights into our men. Not only do the women get brought to the heights of fantastic orgasms (always multiple) through the services of the hero, these gals often get their greatest kicks from playing the love-slave role and serving up all kinds of pleasures to him. At times it takes on the flavor of the serving girls at a Roman orgy plopping grapes in the mouths of their lords and masters. Maybe it's the male need to dominate or a desire to be nurtured, but whatever rests at the psychoanalytic roots of this male fantasy, I think it accounts for the popularity of the "massage parlors" to be found in most major cities. It also accounts for the dreams occidental males have of what they think Japanese geishas provide (but don't). One novelist won my far-out-fantasy-of-the-year award with a scene in which he had four well-endowed, highly aroused young gals, all nude, serving the hero. Two of them are pleasuring every part of his body with every conceivable part of theirs while the third little sexpot is serving him a smorgasbord lunch spread over the bare anatomy of the fourth!

Not only do none of the four become the least bit possessive, they all seem thrilled by the arrangement.

This is one fantasy among several which seems to have little parallel among women. Certainly, there are many gals who enjoy relaxing while they are pleasured all over by their lovers, at least on occasion, but few have fantasies of two or more lovers engaged in a co-operative effort. I don't think this has anything to do with the old business of men being polygamous by nature while women are monogamous (which is probably just another sexual myth anyway). I think it simply comes down to the fact that most women don't want to play Cleopatra surrounded by male love slaves. On the other hand, most of us can be very turned on pleasuring our man those times when he agrees to "just lie back, relax, and enjoy it."

I think if a woman were to write a hard-core erotic novel for women, it would be a one man-one woman love story. There would be sexual variety in it, to be sure, but it would be variety with the same man. Why is it that in the male-oriented novel, the hero runs through, and I do mean *runs through,* at least a half dozen gals, usually of various sizes, shapes, and colors? Frankly, I don't know. Maybe men are more prone to boredom. I know a lot of women who are convinced it means all men are genetically addicted to bed-hopping. Personally, I don't think so. Sure, a lot of men don't stick to one woman, but let's face it, there are also a lot of women playing infidelity games. Maybe men and women are looking for something different and chase around for very different reasons, but I feel certain of one thing: A smart gal who learns about her man, and uses what she learns, can supply all the variety her man might ever desire and all the satisfaction to keep him in her bed.

One final feature to be noted in the hard-core novel: Variety is the spice of success. The writer who can dream up three more unusual ways to have sex or four more unusual locales is sure to hit the pornographic best-seller lists. Doing it standing up on a ferris wheel while covered all over with whipped cream and chocolate syrup is the stuff of which these literary gems are made. Does this mean men are never satisfied unless they have discovered some new acrobatics or another chandelier from which to swing? I don't think so. But this endless quest for variety is too much a part of what is written for men to be ignored. Frankly, from what I've gathered talking to women (as well as my own interests), I think variety adds as much zest to our lives as it does to theirs. More than a minority of our sex, however, are too inhibited to admit it to their men. If they carry it further and turn down any suggestions of new ways and new places, their romance may lose the battle with boredom. Man-pleasuring depends on variety. A talented mistress plays many roles with her man, and she makes a study of the pleasuring techniques which will give him the most so that she can get the most: basic manipulation—*give to get.*

If there is one all-important theme, important, that is, to us, running through all the stacks of sex novels it is this: Every gal is left sexually satisfied by the phenomenal lover-hero. Innocent virgins, confirmed lesbians, and frigid spinsters, all react the same. A single initiation by the virile superman in the joys of heterosexuality and they are left gushing in their gratitude and eager for more. She may have been Miss Modesty herself at the start, but once seduced she abandons her reserve as fast as she sheds her clothes. She unqualifiedly praises her lover's talents, anatomy, and masculinity. And having flowered through this single experience, she is a new woman. She becomes the sexual aggressor. Several pages back, I mentioned the male need to be needed sexually. In the hard-core novels, the women not only get turned-on to sex, they become desperately addicted to it—and to that superman who supplies it.

So far, we have been talking about fantasies. Men enjoy them; so do women. Fantasies and dreams bring some very real satisfactions to living. But what about reality? We do have to live with it and try, as far as possible, to make it conform to our dreams. What if your man isn't the sexual Hercules of the sex novel? Of course, he isn't. No man is. If one turned up, I doubt that any woman would want him. What we want is men, who can make us enjoy being women.

The confident, self-assured lover isn't born; he's carefully developed and nurtured by an intelligent woman. In the days when high-class houses of ill fame were to be found in all major cities, liberal (and affluent) fathers would sometimes take their eighteen- or nineteen-year-old sons down to be introduced to a sympathetic and understanding experienced "girl," to be initiated in the love-making arts. There were, I'm sure, at least a couple of good reasons. First, it was presumed that "nice" girls didn't, and naturally Dad didn't want his son chasing after the not-so-nice kind. If the boy followed Dad's (and certainly Mom's) advice, he stood a good chance of eventually going into marriage with his nervous virginity intact. The wedding night could become a pathetic comedy of errors with the groom not sure of how to put what in where and his naïve and innocent bride left fraught with frustration as the blind attempted to lead the blind. If he was, therefore, to learn anything beyond the distortions and braggings of his fraternity brothers, he had to get some practical experience of "learning by doing." Second, in the brass four-poster bed of the experienced pro, he could perform without feeling any demand to prove something. If she did the job she was hired for, she gave him an abundance of praise, reassurance, and ego-building along with the "instruction." If she was smart, she did her best to convince him he had a natural talent which made him the greatest of lovers, more than enough of a man to make her moan and swoon with pleasure. So a double result was achieved: He learned a sufficient amount about the love-making arts to enable him to confidently guide and initiate his bride when the time came; and his male ego was bolstered enough to greatly reduce, if not eliminate, the honeymoon anxiety which so often leads to the two common male "failures," impotence and premature ejaculation. Even if such elegant "houses" were still around, I doubt many fathers would pay tuition for their son's education at such a school. If they did and Mother found out about it, dear old

Dad might find himself locked up for contributing to the delinquency of a minor! So now, a guy reaches the age at which he's eager to try out the pleasures of the flesh and what does he do? He reads an out-of-date marriage manual his parents had hidden on their closet shelf, tries to remember if there was anything of value he learned in his sex-education classes, concludes there wasn't, goes to a couple of sex movies, and tries to make out with his girlfriend in the back seat of his car. The disaster rate is appalling. In the movies, it had all seemed so easy and casual: one, two, three, and the well-endowed actress stripped to the buff and moved from one position to another like an expert gymnast. There hadn't been all this trouble with bra snaps, and the hero of the movie hadn't had to hassle with a pair of pantyhose beneath a pair of hot pants on a warm night while cramped in a sports car with a girl who kept saying, "What are you *doing?*"

It can get worse. He may get one of those easily shocked little girls who acts like she may faint or vomit when he unzips his fly. Or he may fumble through the whole business only to have her let him know how let down she was. She may burst into tears or anger before, during, or after. She may complain of being hurt physically or emotionally. She may act like she's doing him a big favor. She may even act bored by the whole thing. Here he is, expected to initiate the amorous activities, seduce the coy young thing, and lead her along the path of erotic adventures, and what happens? He fails every step of the way.

There is only one way, in fact, that he can "succeed." She is the one who gives him the pass or fail mark. With the smart, experienced professional in the bordello, every guy who walks through the door is the world's champion lover, and she makes sure he leaves feeling ten feet tall. If his partner doesn't convince a man he is a great, great lover, he will never believe it. And if she doesn't try her best to convince him of it even long before he actually makes it, he never will—at least he won't make it with her (and he just may go looking for a gal who will be bright enough to do the convincing).

There are several ways a gal can use her man's fantasies to the benefit of both of them. All we've touched on so far are some of the more common male sex fantasies which your man may or may not enjoy. If he won't share his own secret thoughts with you, you may have to rely on a knowledge of the "average"; if he won't tell you anything about his taste in food, what can you do except to serve him what you have found most men like? If you can swing it, try to get him to share his fantasies. (You'll probably even find the conversation turns you on, although that isn't your purpose—is it?) You may not have an easy time of it getting him to open up. As we all know, most men have been brainwashed into believing women are easily shocked by even the suggestion of anything that smacks of "far out" sex. If Mother wouldn't have done it, no other woman would listen to such things, or so the reasoning goes. A man has to first be convinced he can share his fantasies without risk of driving his woman into convulsions or a nunnery. This leaves the ball right smack in the lap of his woman. If she has played that "dumb little ole me" role, pretending not to know the meaning of any of those words written on the walls of the girl's room, she may have some *un*convincing to do. (I'll have a few things to say later about the ultimate good sense of employing four-letter words in the right way and in the right place for fun and profit to you.) You might start by suggesting he buy some porno novels for you, or bring out some he may have stashed away. If you have the cool to walk into one of those crummy little shops which sell sex books and magazines (and a variety of battery-operated devices), you might even pick up a few literary works on your own. In addition to providing some enjoyable afternoons, they can serve to break the ice of fantasy sharing. Try suggesting you read to each other and share your observations and reactions. But whatever you do, don't pretend to be the outraged virgin if he tells you that passage about the "harem girl stimulating the Caliph's bodyguard with a lesbian" scene turns him on. If you do, he'll keep his thoughts to himself, and then where are you? As we all know, there has been a lot written about the difference in men and women in how they respond to sexual stimuli. The sex-poll interviewers run around asking gals what turns them on or doesn't; then they compare the answers with what they hear from men. Our sex information used to be based on old wive's tales; now, the researcher takes random samples, then they develop their own old wive's tales. What we all think about and do when the lights are out is one thing. But is it what we are likely to tell some little man with a clipboard and a list of questions? Like devotion to motherhood and the flag, we say what we think is acceptable. So when it comes to sexual stimuli, the members of our sex say what we have been told we are to say. Visual stimuli are not supposed to turn on women. Photographs of nude men, the appearance of our man's erection, pornographic movies, are suppose to leave us cold, or bored, or even disgusted. Those studies reported in the marriage manuals tell us so. Men, on the other hand, are very much aroused by viewing sexual stimuli. And this, we are told, is why *Playboy* and *Penthouse* have large readerships while there are no pin-up magazines for women. Let's say your guy brings home a magazine which is cover-to-cover nothing but naked sex scenes of just about every kind and variety. You can react by (1) telling him how disgusting and ugly you find the photographs; (2) telling him you don't mind him looking at them, but you find them boring and they don't do a thing for you; (3) becoming outraged with jealousy and accusing him of wanting sex with those "cheap whores" who posed for the photographs; or (4) getting turned-on by the pictures and sharing your reactions with him.

If you picked any one of them but (4) you flunked the test. And what if you don't really get turned-on by porno pictures and stores? Well, the first thing you might do is examine your own psyche to discover why not. We gals have been so strongly brainwashed into believing most things sexual leave us cold, we don't let erotic messages get through to whatever part of our brains triggers our urges. With some exposure to sexy material, however, attitudes can change—if, of course, we let them. And why shouldn't we? Sexy feelings are fun! Some of us may have held back on expressing our turned-on feelings out of fear it might scare hell out of men. Maybe this was true in Mother's day, the times they have been changing. Men, as well as women, have been gaining new freedoms, and one of the most important freedoms for all of us is the freedom from sexual stereotypes. I don't think the majority of men want a gal just as cold as the gal who married dear old Granddad. If you find yourself with a guy who wants you to keep your legs as closed as his mind, seduce him into changing his outlook or look elsewhere. By sharing with him those erotic dreams and fantasies you've had, you may encourage him to do the same. How much more imagination you can bring to your love games when you find, for example, that he has had some long-nurtured thoughts of spending an evening with his woman by the fireplace pursuing an artistic interest in mutual body painting. And think of the warm, wet feelings you can experience just talking about it. Doesn't it beat discussions of the weather front!

6
Getting All Dressed Up in the Nude

I know a gal who made love to her man sitting astride him atop an automatic washer. (It was in the spin cycle.) The whole thing was her suggestion, and if there were a sexual consumers' household-hint-of-the-month prize, she'd win my vote. She had the moxey to realize that a gal is apt to get just what she goes after and the female Homo sapiens has a natural creativity in sexual matters which makes her the one best able to set the erotic scenes. Of course, this shatters the tired old sex roles we had pounded into us. Men were the ones supposed to plan the romance and sensuality, weren't they? Why? I listen to women gripe because their men are satisfied to do it every time with the lights out, following the late news, in the missionary position; gals who want the candlelight-and-champagne routine each time but who wear flannel pajamas to bed and beer-can hair curlers to greet their men. If we want the excitement kept in and the boredom kept out, we can't expect the responsibility to fall totally on our men. We have more time and inclination to think about romance and all the fun trappings of sensualism than they do. Plus we have our feminine imagination.

We also have something else going for us: We have the major say in most things which go to make up a sensual environment, for them as well as for us. Sure, we go for that private beach he finds and that late evening fire he builds in the fireplace after the shower-à-deux, but we gals set most of the scenes and create most of the turn-ons. When you come right down to it, seduction is primarily a female art. A man works hard at the business of bedding a gal, but we know what every woman knows: Females work and scheme with everything they've got to manipulate men into manipulating them into lovely compromising positions.

The first environment to develop in our seductive art is *his woman*. That's obvious, isn't it? Every normal, man-loving girl wants the same thing: She wants to be wanted by men—especially by that one special man. It's fun, isn't it, seeing him get an erection while watching you cross you legs in a way that "carelessly" shows a glimpse of black panties? The more we can throw the switch on those male hormones of his, the more we can feel like women. And I mean a turn-on, not a tease. The water bed, mirrored ceiling, and colored lighting in the boudoir play their part, but the gal who plays her seductive cards right can make her guy want to disrobe her on a municipal bus or ravish her in the main reading room of the public library. And after all, that's what is important.

When you walk through a hotel lobby with him, do the bell-men and desk clerk run their eyes over your hills and valleys? It's a great feeling, right? And if they don't? Life can be a real downer, right? But how does your man feel about it? A very insecure man might wish he could turn you into a plucked turkey, but a normal guy with confidence in his own masculine abilities will enjoy every lecherous glance you attract. What guy doesn't want to be able to say, "Eat your heart out," to the rest of the male fraternity? Sure it's part of that male ego of his. I suppose along with fast sports cars, par golf, the top-of-the-corporation pecking order, and the greatest muscles and most impressive penis in the locker room, a really sexy-looking gal on his arm is a status symbol. The womens libbers would say such a gal is being exploited, degraded, and viewed only as a sex object (ignoring the fact that at least half the militant feminists view other *females* as sex objects). At least she has a man who is interested in *her*, who sees her as sexy and capable of turning on other men as well as himself. And what gal's vanity doesn't get a boost from that, assuming she is heterosexual and likes men?

Let me quickly say I don't for a minute believe men want their women sexy-looking primarily to win one-upmanship games with other men. Maybe there are a few kooks who do, but they are very few. The masculine pride he takes in you is the whipped cream with the cherry on top. The satisfying main course is what he gets from you when the two of you are alone. Whether you play your sex games atop the automatic washer or with the aid of snorkel tubes in the swimming pool, when you finally get down to business, it is that body of yours—and what you do with it— which tops the list of what turns him on. It's the prime stimulus in his erotic environment. So let's start by talking about our female bodies from the skin out.

There is only so much, and no more, most of us can do with the bodies we have, but it is often quite a bit. And with the aid of science, the cosmetics industry, and some imagination, we can now work a score of minor miracles to correct the mistakes Mother Nature and our genes handed us. If we have one certain man we have staked a claim on, then good old-fashioned self-interest dictates the approach: We want to keep tuned-in to his turn-ons. The gal with a 32A bust whose guy digs "youthful, early teen-age" would be out of her gourd to run down and get a silicone implant pushing her out to 46D. The gal who says, "I dress and makeup to please only myself," is either a misogamist or a moron. And the gal who doesn't study every square inch of her body with a view to its turn-on value to him doesn't want to keep her man very much. Or at least she doesn't want him climbing into her bed in the same state of maleness I like to see in my man.

I'm not going to go into a long discussion of skin care, how to apply eyeliner, and what to do with those excess pounds. There are enough books on those subjects to fill a library. Some are good; some not. Needless to say, every smart gal keeps up on the latest ideas and develops an expertise in emphasizing the best she has to offer. Men are visual creatures when it comes to sex.

The average guy never tires of looking at females in the nude, whether photographs in girlie magazines, plaster statues atop Las Vegas hotel fountains, or topless dancers. And every red-blooded, man-loving gal never tires of displaying herself in a state of undress to her man. If every gal in the world had the figure she would like to have, swimsuits would drop like leaves in autumn on every beach. We females are exhibitionists to the core. Only two things keep any of us from baring everything every chance we get: some crippling hangups where sex is concerned, and/or, a big let-down feeling when we stand in the buff before a full-length mirror. Whichever the cause, the gal who stays covered up with her man is robbing herself of a lot of good healthy fun. Not the least of which is observing his reactions to her body.

If those dull old inhibitions that were laid on you and me when we were ready for our first training bra are still with you, isn't it time to shed them? No man wants a gal who holds back, covers up, and plays the convent-school virgin ten years after she's lost her maidenhead. The woman who sleeps in a nightgown or pajamas, who doesn't enjoy lifting her breasts up and down brushing her hair, sitting nude before her dressing table, while her man looks on, the gal who doesn't experience a warm thrill somewhere between her waist and her knees as she feels her man's eyes on her when she moves her nakedness across the room toward him, isn't alive to men; and she's dead to her womanhood. If this is your problem, adopt a decidedly feminine rallying cry: "Nudity Is Nice." Start spending all the time you can in the nude. If there is no one else around the house or apartment during the day (except him, of course), do your thing, whatever it is, in the altogether. There are only a few experiences more delicious than the feel of nothing but the air on skin all over. As you walk by the mirrors, practice standing and moving in ways which show off what you have to its best advantage. (If you don't like a bulge here and there, get to work on a reshaping program, but don't waste time on any "I'm so ugly" handwringing just because you don't have the most bountiful breasts or the perkiest fanny in town. Remember, with practice and talent, you can make beautiful music even on a slightly beat-up old piano.) When it comes to sex, body language should be a woman's second native tongue. The gal who communicates well with her body says, "I dig sex, with a capital SEX, and I have no reluctance about admitting it." She develops the technique of moving her pelvis with a ball-bearing movement in which her hips move in a fluid back-and-forth swing (the way that Mother told us we shouldn't). She learns how to move her shoulders in a to-and-fro movement which gives her breasts an "I want to be pleasured" appeal. There is simply no way the movements can be put into words, but I am firmly convinced there isn't a woman alive who doesn't know what that fluid, "I want sex," movement is. I don't mean the phony Mae West or Marilyn Monroe swagger. That sort of fanny-swinging is more a caricature of sexuality than the real thing. And it is also narcissistic. Those kind of females leave you with the impression they would use a mirrored ceiling in the bedroom to check if their hair setting was in place! The genuinely sensuous woman enjoys her body and what she can do with it. And her movements communicate this very clearly.

For a gal with a seductive mentality, nudity with her lover should never be a matter of simply running around with no clothes on. Clumping across the bedroom floor with an "I'm on my way to brush my teeth and pare my toenails" expression and gait can be less than a turn-on. The flat-footed walk makes a girl's legs and fanny look dumpy and no woman should walk in the nude the way Mrs. Housewife wanders through the supermarket. The sexy mistress doesn't stand, sit, walk, or recline in the nude. She *poses!* Like a skilled actress, she studies her best sides, the most effective ways to move her hips, swing her legs, arch her back, and lift her arms. Sexiness in a woman is 50 per cent state of mind and 50 per cent learned skills. If you're not sure of your skills in posing, try practicing before a full-length mirror when he isn't around. If you already have the skills down pat, well, additional practice never hurts. Besides, it's kind of fun.

In addition to keeping your figure in the shape he finds exciting, there are a few things you can do to enhance its appeal. First, and most obvious, get rid of the unwanted body hair and keep it off. Most of us shave our legs (or use a depilatory), but those stubbles have a way of cropping back up awfully fast. No gal wants her man to feel sandpaper when he rubs his hand or cheek over her calves. Checking during each daily bath should avoid that uncomfortable "caught with the stubbles" feeling when you're lying beside him. The same goes for underarm hair unless you or your man is European and/or finds underarm hair erotic. Some of us have additional problems with body hair. Some women sprout a few hairs around the border of the areola (the pigmented area surrounding the nipple). Most men find this unappealing, so if you have this problem, it would be a smart idea to remove them. (Since there are generally only a few, this shouldn't present much problem.) Some gals also find they have a line of hairs extending from the navel to the pubic hair. In this day of bikinis, gals with such unwanted growths usually tackled this removal problem way back when they bought their first grown-up swimsuit, but if you still have such adornment, get rid of it. That kind of body hair is sexy only on a male. As for pubic hair itself, I think most gals just ignore it. We shouldn't. After years of airbrushing the pubic hair off center-fold photos, the top men's magazines have taken a bold step toward hirsute liberation. Now, blonde, brunette, or redhead curls adorn the triangle formerly obliterated in the photographic darkroom. Now, every reader of the magazine knows what her hairdresser knows (unless she's had a second color rinse). Thanks to some enlightened courts, male readers can now enjoy photographs of gals who are natural rather than neutered. While there are some men who are turned-on by a shaved pubic area (whether for variety or some other reason, and if your man expresses an interest in seeing you without the curls, why not get out that razor and give him an adventure), most men have preferences in color, shape, and style of hair beneath the lace bikinis. While there is no hair restorer to help you out if your man is one who digs a massive bush of curls and your hair dis-

tribution is on the scanty side, there is something you can do if
you have a mound of hair which grows as long and untidy as a
string mop. Some of the exclusive salons of beauty offer wax
hair-removal treatments including what they usually call a "bikini" (the purpose, of course, being to eliminate the hair which
might peek from under the edges of a skimpy suit; show girls
and dancers have long made "around the edges" hair removal a
regular professional routine). Personally, I don't think one has to
go into a high-priced hair remover to take care of what is usually
a fairly minor beauty routine. Most of us can shave our own legs,
our own underarms, and our own you-know-what's. On the other
hand, I've never tried the wax "bikini" treatment. Maybe I'm
missing something. Whatever method of hair removal you employ, keep a couple of things in mind: Unless you remove the
hair follicle (or it dies), hair grows back. If you don't tend to it
as you do in keeping your legs smooth, you may find yourself
itching with a five-day stubble, and worse yet, he may find himself getting rubbed the wrong way—painfully. And the other
point: Watch what you're doing down there. I don't see how
this could happen unless she was standing on her head while she
wielded the clippers, but I read in one medical column a word
of caution that hair clippings might enter the vagina if care
isn't taken, and problems could result. For whatever it's worth,
maybe it's well to be aware of.

With the unnecessary and unwanted hair off, concentrate
on keeping that skin of yours in tiptop erotic condition. Commercials for dishwashing detergents plug away for hand softness.
We spend fortunes on clays, creams, and lotions designed to pre-
serve our faces. But aside from attention to scaly elbows and
rough, red knees, we often neglect the rest of our skin surface.
It doesn't make much sense, does it? Our men are touching a lot
of places on us besides our faces, hands, and elbows. Hopefully,
they're touching us all over. As every gal probably has discovered,
most men thoroughly enjoy exploring female flesh (and what
woman doesn't experience pure ecstasy under the stroking of
her lover?), but the exploration urge can be increased or de-

creased by what a woman does to enhance her skin. A woman's skin should look and feel sensuous, warm, soft, and smooth. Her calves and arms should be as silken to the touch as her breasts. There are several good body lotions on the market. Sample them, select one which does the most for you, and lavish it on and into your skin every day. If you have time before love-making, give yourself some additional lotioning. Your skin should be left with that soft tropics feel to it; not greasy, so be sure to rub it in or remove any excess. Body oils or lotions have their place in love-making, and we'll be talking about it later, but here we are talking about the "natural" skin he loves to touch—all over.

Skin pigmentation, or color, can also be used to a turn-on advantage. Maybe you've noticed how often those centerfold models are "well tanned" with some bare-minimum, milky-white areas where the bikini had been before she revealed all to the readers. I, for one, have wondered whether they were all legitimately tanned, or if some psychologically shrewd photographer did some work with body makeup. No difference. The effect is the important thing. Those white bikini areas standing out against bronze skin provide an extra erotic stimulation to many men. Maybe it's that "Here's that part of me I'm uncovering just for you" message, a sort of forbidden-fruit enticement, which does it, but who cares. All I know, or need to know, is that those "tan marks" come across sexy. At least it has enough effect on most men to make some planned tanning important. Whatever you do, don't wear a swimsuit which gives you a bizarre "crisscrossed by straps and chains" look when you lie in the sun. Some suits may look sexy as a haremful of Raquel Welches when paraded by the pool, but if you spread yourself for a few hours in the sun in them, they can leave you looking as if you've been branded with a waffle iron. And that just *isn't* sexy. Keep the minimum part of your breasts and that skimpy bikini section across your hips, front and back, white. Let all the rest of you tan. If you don't live in an area where you can tan all year round and can't get a tan which will last until the following summer, maybe you can try some of that body makeup from time to time. Put on a strapless bra and bikini panties and apply the makeup (it will wash off the garments) in a "well-tanned" marking. The rewards may be well worth the effort.

During one of the more enlightened, and fun, periods of prerevolutionary France, ladies at court were said to apply rouge to their nipples and surrounding areas and to wear gowns which exposed same to the gaze of the male nobility. We can learn something from them. Unless we happen to be blond (and haven't yet gone through a pregnancy, since that seems to make a difference), our nipples and areola are apt to be brownish and perhaps not the most "alive" color. What the ladies of the French court knew is that the nipples and their surrounding area are at their prettiest when they are the color of the lips: pink and full of life. There usually isn't reason to makeup your nipples each morning as you would your lips (if you have reason, lucky you), but if you are bathing and doing things to yourself in preparation for *him,* brushing on some pink lip coloring or a blush over the nipple and areola is one way to enhance your body beautiful. For variety, you might even try some of the darker or brighter red shades of lipstick for the same decorative purpose, but unless you're going in for the more far-out body painting, which we will get into later, don't experiment with bizarre shades. Unless he's from outer space, I don't think he'll be turned on by a pair of protruding green nipples.

Another thing you might try for interest: beauty marks. Those ladies of the court with their high-piled powdered wigs were always pictured with a carefully placed spot high on a cheekbone. They have reappeared in fashion every few decades since. In recent years we have been able to buy paste-on beauty marks in all sorts of shapes and colors, stars, crescents, zodiac signs, and they can be fun for a touch of the exotic. But beauty marks don't have to be restricted to the face only. I haven't done any surveys of my own, but from a couple of articles I've read recently, the tattoo artist, who used to earn his living decorating the chests and forearms of sailors on shore leave, may soon move his inks and needles into a corner of a Beverly Hills high-couture salon and hang out a "Ladies Only" sign. And yes, I am serious. It seems some of the more adventurous gals are having their bodies adorned with tattoos, usually in some spot not likely to be suntanned. Not that the gals are following the old salts with skulls and daggers and "Death Before Dishonor." They go for something strictly feminine with more than a touch of sexiness. It might be a rosebud on the side of the buttocks or a small cluster of cherries high enough on the inner thigh to be covered by a bikini (if that's possible). Some have gone for that circle with the pointed male sex symbol in the same spot, and quite a few have decorated their private anatomy with their lover's name (a choice many a sailor lived to regret when love during an evening of boozing proved less than enduring). All I can say for such anatomical art work is, "To every gal her own thing." As for me, the thoughts of somebody with needles fooling around those parts of me is enough to keep me unmarked by anything but my vaccination. Besides, whatever turn-on value such adornments might have would probably be largely owing to their value as sexual variety, and tattoos are put on to stay. His reaction when he discovers that strategically placed rosebud could, nevertheless, be highly gratifying. And, as the commercials say, "Today, no woman has to slave away over or under a hot tattoo needle." Body decals of a variety of designs, which look very much like expert tattoos and which peel off without trouble, are available in smart boutiques and cosmetic departments. They might not yet be carried in your corner chain drugstore, but with some shopping around you should be able to turn them up. If not, well you can always pick up some poster paints and do some surprise art work of your own.

I said I wasn't going to give any advice on cosmetics and hairstyle, and I'm not. But I can't resist making one point of importance to every gal with a genuine interest in getting the best of loving from her man. The time for loving is not the time to look your worst. Now, unless we're trying to turn off our men, we all know that, but we also know the problem. Most sex goes on after the TV goes off. And who wants to get up afterward to cream off makeup and peel off eyelashes? No woman I know. Sleep all night every night in foundation, eyeliner, and the rest, and soon you can have skin with the texture of old army boots, as every one of us is aware. There are a couple of tricks and compromises, however, which will keep a gal's skin intact without having her greet her lover looking like a patient in the recovery room. As they say about the magicians, "It's all done with mirrors"; only in this magic, it's done with lights.

We plan our makeup, of course, for the lighting as well as the color of our clothes, hair, and perhaps the room in which we will be "performing" during the day and evening. The makeup best for that luncheon date on the terrace will seldom show up best in that intimate oak-paneled French restaurant for the after-theater supper by candlelight. In the boudoir (or wherever you choose for the loving), use your lighting to substitute for makeup. Candlelight is the most obvious. I'm sure every female has learned, by at least the age of twelve, what nice things candlelight can do for her skin tones. No woman should be without two or three candles carefully placed in her erotic environments. It isn't always convenient, however, to light the candles, so some artificial lighting which will do a comparable job is called for. Soft pink lighting is best for most of us. If you want to try some color mixing which may work well, try combinations of blue and red bulbs. Blue bulbs alone can sometimes be interesting. If they are not too blue, they may provide a soft "moonlight" effect, but try out the effects before your mirror. Excessive blue and you may look a bit macabre. Pure red lighting and your natural coloring gets washed out. Whatever you do, don't go for yellows or greens. White light isn't much better no matter how dim it may be, but if you must have incandescent bulbs in your sex nest, keep the number few and the wattage low. Actually, I can't see why love-making would have to be illuminated by white light (and I'm not saying I see no reason for *some* lighting: we all know it's fun to enjoy a visual turn-on). If reading in bed is your thing or your man's, those little "individual" reading lamps which give a narrow beam of light work fine without flooding the room with something resembling the lighting in an examination room. Whatever you do, keep any fluorescent lights turned off. Those vanity mirrors with a ring of fluorescent lights or a couple of fluorescent tubes on the sides are great for the fine touches of eye and lip makeup, but don't leave that light on when you get ready to make the big scene with him. It does terrible things to a woman.

With the proper lighting, the makeup problem is solved. Leave your eyebrow coloring on along with your lipstick and eyeliner and lashes (or reapply them after removing your makeup). You can easily remove the lashes and place them on the headboard or night stand afterward when the lights are out. The lighting will do the rest, and you can sleep with the eyeliner, brow darkening, and lipstick without skin damage.

As for the hair, wouldn't we all rather climb into bed with our head in a flour sack than with our head covered with curlers. At least if we have a man waiting in the bed! I am absolutely convinced that those women who greet their men looking like some creature in search of a head transplant have a deep and abiding hatred of men and a pathetic deficiency in those good feminine feelings. Some of us, however, do feel forced to mechanize our heads from time to time in order to look glamorous the next morning. Perhaps it doesn't have to be. With a bit of study of hairstyles (that appeal to him, of course), a style can be found which won't demand that overnight ugliness. Every girlie magazine gives testimony to the fact that most men are turned on by long hair, especially when it's cascaded over a pillow. Your man may like your hair cropped short when he introduces you to the boss's wife, but find out what he likes when the lights are low and you step out of that transparent baby doll. In her survey of the sexual mores of contemporary wives, *The Erotic Life of the American Wife* (Delacorte Press, 1972), Natalie Gittleson quotes one unhappy married male's definition of a nymphomaniac: "A girl who has her hair done and agrees to make love with her husband on the same day." To which I would add my definition of a frigid *Hausfrau:* "A girl who has her hair done and *refuses* to make love with her husband on the same day." I might even go so far as to define a semifrigid wife as "A girl who doesn't do her hair in hopes of making love to her husband." Today we are in luck. Wigs, falls, and other hair accessories are available in every color, style, and price range. They go a long way toward sparing us that pin and curler ordeal. And surprising him with long tresses of a hue different from your own may add a plus to the love-making for both of you.

From the first time she disrobes for a man, a woman should have an erotic wardrobe, selected with care and a knowledge of male psychology. Unfortunately, to that long list of things Mother never, never taught us, most of us could include a knowledge of sex fashions. It's ten to one or better Mother herself didn't know anything about it, or if she did, she didn't make use of it. Man-pleasuring wasn't the thing for Mother's generation of females. So we have to learn it all by ourselves.

Like keeping a foxy-looking figure, it's often more what you get rid of than what you keep when it comes to a provocative wardrobe. We can be safe in starting with a basic assumption: Just about everything designed for women falls short of being sexy. I don't know whether all those Seventh Avenue faggots designing women's fashions are really that anti-woman, but I do know this: A woman has no easy time finding apparel to wear next to her skin which makes her feel sensuous and which raises the ardor of her man. They can be found, however. First, toss out all those pieces of undergarments which don't turn on his switch. And what are they? Some are obvious, aren't they? Nightgowns are first on the list! No woman with her sex drive headed in the right direction would ever—and I do mean ever wear one of those missionary muumuus to bed. The woman who wears nothing to bed but several carefully placed drops of Chanel No. 5 has the right idea about nightwear. When the lights go out, a woman wants to feel skin against skin, nothing else. But before that, exotic lingerie, designed for taking off, can help bring a woman—and her man—to where she wants to be: curled in his arms, melted in contentment.

While throwing out nightgowns and pajamas, eliminate those good "practical" white and pink panties and bras, the ones which don't give off any sexual messages. Black bras and black bikini panties may be an old sex stereotype, but if they still have a way of triggering a male response, why should we declare them "out of vogue"? Since pantyhose came in, we can wear the shortest skirts or the skimpiest hot pants without fussing over what may be showing. But this has not been an unmixed advantage. On a breezy day, men used to watch us long and lustily in hopes of catching a glimpse of white thigh or perhaps something more. Now there's no point to it. They know what they're going to see: nothing but nylon. Like body shirts, leotards, and half-slips, pantyhose have their place, but sexy in the bedroom they are *not*. Maybe the sexiest bras and panties won't do the most for your figure in the dress you wear when you meet him for cocktails, but there is no rule saying you can't do a quick change into underthings calculated to interest him before you drop your negligee in the bedroom. I don't know why, but a black lace half-bra together with a black garter belt and hose is what the experts call *erotogenic*, meaning it gets the desired rise out of most men. Leave off the panties, of course. And when it comes to negligees, shorties, harem pants, and other such behind-closed-doors apparel, shop with care—and an eye to what effect you're hoping for. None of those too-cute fluffy things. He isn't looking for Little Bo-peep. And shy away from those pristine wedding-night negligees. You know the kind I mean. They drape them on the mannequins in the better stores at Christmas. ("She'll just love it; lime green is very popular this season.") They're designed, I think, for the Ice Maiden in a coronation scene. Hopeful husbands have been giving them to hostile wives for years. What a smart woman looks for is something which gives her man even more raunchy ideas, not less. And no one but a neurotic wants to play modesty games and hide what we want them to seek.

What goes for those near-transparent things we shed when we climb into bed with him also goes for what we wear in the morning, afternoon, and when he takes us to meet his ninety-year-old grandmother: If it isn't something which makes him want to take it off, forget it. As we all know, this can be a real challenge. "Who do women dress for?" has been a question argued for more years than any of us has been buying clothes. I don't have the answer for all women, or even most women, but I know that if I want to manipulate my man into pleasuring me, I'll dress in a way to pleasure him—and give him ideas. At times, this can have a woman walking a fashion tightwire of taste, male sensitivity, and seduction. Our men want us to look sexy, but few want to walk through a hotel lobby with a gal who looks as if she has a lease on the third bar stool from the end. He may do more than a double-take when some stacked filly poured into a black silk slashed down to the navel and slit up the hip swings by, but when it comes to his woman, well, how many men want to be seen in daylight with a lady of the night?

Clothes with subtle sex are never easy to find, but somewhere between that tweedy look of women convention delegates and the poured-into look of a topless dancer between shows, there are clothes which bring out the sensual *you*, and in a way which communicates to *him*. Not necessarily to all men. Men are not all alike any more than women are. But it is one man who is most important, and he is the one you aim for. If you know his turn-ons very, very well, you may know that special outfit when you see it, but that calls for a lot of "knowing." It's much simpler, isn't it, to just let him pick your clothes? Why not? And before you decide I'm somewhere out of my senses, let me assure you I know the usual reason why not. Few of our men are overly enthusiastic when we drag them into a dress shop. And who can blame them. The average man doesn't shop like the average woman. We go out shopping, and the shopping is half the fun. They go out to buy something when they decide they need it, but the fun of shopping is a kick which escapes him. At the same time, they want us dressed in clothes *for them*. So if he's reluctant, try this: Let him know, in very explicitly loving terms, that you want to wear clothes which will have a turn-on value to him, and you want him to pick them out. If you show him you mean it, it just might be enough to get him to go along. I'll have more to say of this later.

7
Rub-a-dub-dub, One Man in a Tub

For getting a man in that relaxed and tranquil mood so conducive to sex, nothing beats a relaxing bath for openers. One administered by his woman, that is. Many couples make a frequent thing of showering together and many enjoy sharing a tub, but since we are directing our interest in these pages to man-pleasuring, let's begin with some talk about giving him the benefit of your expert services in bathing him.

We gals need to understand that few men enjoy bathing. I'm not saying men bathe less often than women or that they have a twelve-year-old's aversion to washing behind their ears or that they like walking around smelling like three-day-worn sweat socks. I'm saying they don't find *pleasure* in their bath. Our female sex is something else again. Any gal with the right amount of feminine narcissism (one who enjoys her body as she should) has learned to make her bath a major sensory experience. She uses water softeners, bubble bath, and bath oils. She fills a tub to the brim, leans her head back against an air pillow, and luxuriates herself by the hour. A warm bath *cum* masturbation has become the afternoon ritual for the contemporary housewife. And the soap operas can't begin to compete. But I'm not telling you anything new, am I? Not so with a man, however. The average guy is more apt to take a shower than a bath, and aside from the showers he takes with his woman, he seldom makes it a sensual experience of much fun. In fact, a lot of the poor devils even seem to have some masochistic tendencies. They finish it off by turning it to ice water and climbing out blue and shaking. But seldom, if ever, do they indulge themselves in a deep bath with the oils and all. I can't climb inside the male mind to tell you why with any certainty, but I can make an educated guess. That is, I hope it's educated (at least it's experienced). I think men have been conditioned to think self-pleasuring is unmasculine. It's the old machismo bit. Enter the bullfight and have a horn driven through your tummy and you've proven your masculinity. Freeze your dignity and a few other things in a duck blind and you have shown the world you have gonads. Reclining in a tub of warm water and feeling the nice things the water does to the skin surface, however, is questionable. I'll bet a lot of guys have the idea that silks, satin sheets, and warm baths might mark them as pansies. Whatever the reason, not many men make a pleasurable ritual of a bath.

Ah, but they would if their women served up special baths in the manner only a sensuous woman can. If you haven't tried it, by all means do. It can work wonders. The first time, however, you may have to seduce him into it (or persuade him, or coax him). Don't ask him if he wants to be bathed. He may feel embarrassed, guilty, or simply that you have blown your wig. Draw his bath before you tell him about it. Set the scene, then issue the invitation.

The Deep Bath: This is designed for pure relaxation, a soaking away of all tensions. You've probably spent many a lazy afternoon dreaming away the time in a deep bath. Next to great sex, it's the closest thing to sheer bliss. The first step is to set the scene. Next to the bedroom, the bathroom should be the most carefully designed room in the house. It should be a room designed for everything sensual. You know, sunken six-foot-square tub built for two, a glass wall with a view of the ocean, and a sun deck, built-in stereo, and carpeting of sealskin. Alas, the architects and home builders are probably no more sensual in their inclinations and designs than the average undertaker, so we don't see many such bathrooms. And then there is the practical consideration called money. The bathroom of my dreams would cost as much as the average two-bedroom house. So I have to be satisfied with something less—much less—which means the typical bathroom, no view, no sun deck, and only as much sensuality as I can put into it. But that's quite a bit when I plan to give my man a bath.

First of all, the usual white light is strictly out. The bath is intended to tranquilize, and white light isn't tranquil. You might get a small lamp and blue, pink, or amber bulbs to plug in for bathing. Or if you want the greatest of turn-ons, candlelight in the bathroom is it.

Next, make sure that bathroom of yours is not the hair-in-the-sink, towels-on-the-floor mess that is so common. Sadly, most of us pay a lot more attention to the appearance of our living room and kitchen than to the bathroom or even the bedroom. It's a sad misordering of values. Fix up that bathroom to make it a room with appeal—sex appeal. Why not tropical plants and incense? And how about a supply of man-sized bath towels? Pour in the bath oil before you start running the water, and don't skimp on the amount of oil. Give some thought, however, to the fragrance. You may be crazy over a very sweet floral scent, but it may not be his thing—except when you're wearing it. Oils can now be found in just about every fragrance imaginable. Fill the tub to just short of overflowing, warm, but not so hot he has to climb in an inch at a time. You don't want to parboil him. If it's too hot, he will be totally limp in more ways than one when he climbs out and/or he won't be able to stay in very long, and a deep bath should be a lengthy one.

By all means, suit the desires of your man, but unless he wants it, leave the soap out entirely, and that also goes for washcloths. The purpose of this deep bath is pleasuring and relaxing, not washing. Bubble bath can be fun for your afternoon bath, but all those soap bubbles can just get in the way when you're bathing him. Besides, they can leave a soap film all over him when you towel him off that isn't as nice a feeling as the bath oil (and doesn't taste as good).

Now starts the fun part. You have the bath all in readiness before you invite him in. It can be even more fun if you can surprise him with it. (Of course, if you've never spent much time pleasuring him in the past, he may decide you've lost your wits. In shock, he may drown.) Insist that you undress him. No matter what he says, that's *your* privilege. And make the undressing a major production. Take your time, lots of time, and demonstrate with your hands and your lips (but play it kind of cool; you don't want things to go too fast) that his body is more touchable than a mink coat (and certainly a lot more erotic!).

After he steps in the tub, you can slip off your negligee. (After all, you don't want to get it wet, do you?) Kneel or sit beside the tub.

This is a great time for talk, especially talk of love and romance. Let him lie back and relax. Gradually, you can add hot water, but be sure you never let it get so hot you wipe him out. After he has a chance to unwind all those muscles and let that warmth seep into his pores, you can begin your underwater massage.

Move your hands under water over his body. In this, the technique is based upon the movement of water. As you move your hands, the water moves ahead of them in underwater waves. Let the movement of the water massage him. You don't have to massage his muscles, or whatever, directly with your hands, or at least not with any pressure. It's best to keep your hands about a quarter of an inch from his skin with your hands cupped, pushing the water up along his skin surface. If you cup your hand and push the water up between his legs in a way that it moves and stimulates his penis and testicles, you can provide him a sensory experience which is truly fabulous (to quote the man I look to for "consultation"). Personally, I find it best to not come on too strong in sexual aggressiveness in administering a bath, or for that matter, in any approaches to my lover (unless, of course, he has given the signals which say he is in the mood for me to be "aggressive"—which is something else again). If he gets the idea you are giving him a bath or massage or whatever as a sort of sexual demand for performance, he may have one very devil of a time raising his ardor and/or anything else. The idea is to relax him, take away all those tensions of the day. If he gets the idea you are simply pursuing your own desires and using the bath as a means to an end—your end—you may strike out. If you want a suggestion for a worth-while investment, let me put in a plug for one of those whirlpool-bath machines which swirl the water all around the bath and can direct the underwater current in whatever direction you choose. It turns a bath into an aquatic massage, delightful for him, fantastic for you.

Whatever you do, don't let him get out of the tub too soon. No matter how much he may be used to those five-minute baths and showers or how turned-on he may be by your pleasuring, put your foot down and insist he lie back and soak his cares away. A half hour should be the minimum and an hour, with warm water added from time to time, is not too long. You might encourage him to relax with his eyes shut while you read to him from a book of erotic prose.

When he steps from the bath, there is another big plus you can have waiting. Place a chair, covered with a deep pile towel, beside the tub and have him sit down while you pat him dry. He can stay loose, relaxed, and aroused, while you do all sorts of delicious things to him. Where the two of you go from there is up to the imaginations and desires of both of you, but whatever happens, you can be sure it will be worth the effort and the loving you put into that bath.

The Body Shampoo: This is an experience which is pure fun for both of you. You can give him a body shampoo; he can give one to you. A body shampoo is part washing and part massage. And it's a treat that should not be missed by any loving couple.

Prepare your shampoo before you begin. For this, you can use a scented liquid soap, which is fabulous but usually expensive. You might try a baby shampoo, diluted with water of course, or a liquid dishwashing soap, the kind which are advertised as kind to your hands (not liquid detergent). If you like it fragrant, you might try adding some bath oil or essence. Mix your shampoo in a bowl, warmed of course. And for the body shampoo, make sure the bathroom is considerably warmer than usual. I'm sure your man doesn't want a frigid bathroom any more than he wants a frigid woman. And for a body shampoo, it's doubly important because he isn't going to be immersed in warm water.

Yes, that's what I said. A body shampoo is not a bath; it's a shampoo. You can give it to your lover while he is reclining in the tub. If this is your choice, run warm water over the bottom of the tub first, to take the chill off that cold surface. The two of you may prefer having him sit on a stool or recline on a bath mat. Dip your hands in the shampoo lotion and begin. (You can, of course, pour it on him a small amount at a time, but personally I find it kind of hard to handle; I get too much and it runs all over.) Lather him all over. But take your time, plenty of time. You might start, for example, with one of his hands. Work a rich lather on his palm, the back of his hand, and his fingers one by one. Then work your way up his arm, over his shoulders, and down the other arm. Every so often you will have to dip your hands in the water; a thick soap solution can begin to dry and get sticky.

When you have him shampooed all over—sparing no part of that wonderful body of his—it's time for a rinse. Here you will need one of those shampoo hose attachments for the tub or, if you're in the shower, one of those telephone shower attachments. Turn the water up full and rinse him from head to toe with the shower nozzle held close to his skin. The tingling feeling should bring him alive all over.

If you want to give him an outstanding variation on the body shampoo, try this: Lather him with a pair of fur mitts on your hands, the kind of mitts with the fur on the outside. Some specialty shops carry them, and they're even available in some automobile accessory stores (they're used in washing cars—how dull!). With lots of suds and soft fur, you can serve up an unparalleled experience in sensuality.

You, a Bar of Soap, and Him: To suggest that couples might try showering together would be a little like suggesting weiners be eaten with sauerkraut. Everyone has already tried it. And every couple has already discovered its advantages. But there are a couple of things you may not have tried which can add to that cozy shower stall for two. For one thing, you might try placing a kitchen stool in the shower, or even a straight-backed chair if it will fit. (I'm afraid a chair with any kind of padding might become a bit soggy and not much fun to sit on the next morning, so maybe you better skip the overstuffed ones.) In a chair or seated on a stool, he can sit back and relax while you lather and rinse him. And of course, he can do the same for you. Furthermore, while you can make love in a standing position in a shower stall, a stool adds the seated positions to the sexual repertoire. The shower does offer one distinct advantage for a body shampoo. Since he is standing, you can easily shampoo his body both front and back with no limits on where you can reach. And with a flexible shower attachment, the same goes for rinsing him. If you do have a flexible shampoo or "telephone" attachment, try making love sometime, taking turns spraying one another's body while you are so delightfully "engaged." Even without such an attachment, making love while a hard spray of water from the showerhead pelts the two of you can be an extra stimulating experience. One of my favorite fantasies is making love outdoors during a tropical rain squall, perhaps on a beach in Hawaii, on the deck of a houseboat in the Caribbean, or beside the pool overlooking the bay of Acapulco. One of these days I'll get the chance. I've been promised.

And here's another great idea. In Sapporo, Japan, the gals who serve the male customers in the bathhouses practice a technique of body shampoo which is pure feminine genius. The girl, in the nude of course, lathers her own body all over.

Rubbing, moving, and squirming her body against his, she then proceeds to "wash" him. The customer can even employ a couple of girls if he feels in need of a particularly thorough washing down. Try it. You can count on a more than favorable response from him. And for you? The experience can only be described as indescribable.

While not strictly a bath, I want to include the increasingly popular sauna bath in this chapter since it belongs in the book, and I can't think of anyplace else to put it. A few years ago, most of us had never heard of a sauna. Or if we had, we knew it as a practice of some rugged Scandinavians who first cooked themselves red as lobsters in a steam boiler while flagellating themselves with switches and finished the ritual off, risking a heart attack, by plunging into a snowbank or icy lake. Not today. Sauna bathing may not be as popular today as, say, second television sets, but a large number of men and women have been recruited to the ranks of sauna supporters in the last five years. Sauna baths have been installed in hotels, health spas, massage parlors, and most important to most of us, in homes and apartments. Sad to say, I haven't come across any private saunas for two in hotels and health spas, and we don't all have either the space or the money to install one at home. If you do, however, take advantage of it. To use your sauna alone, when you could make the scene together, is sad or insane; take your pick. Your sauna is a great place for relaxing, letting all the kinks work out through your pores, communicating—both verbally and non-verbally, and pleasuring one another. Making love in the steam heat of your sauna may not be your thing for every evening, but try it for variety; it can be an exciting variation.

And speaking of hot and cold sensations, here is a little gimmick you might try: Let him take his bath or shower first so he is ready and waiting for you. Then climb into a deep, hot bath by yourself. And make sure it is hot, as hot as you can take it in comfort. Don't stay in too long, however, or you may pass out before you make it to the loving. While you lie there soaking in that bath-oil-scented water, spread your legs apart. By the time you step from the tub, your skin surface will be several degrees above normal, and your sensitive female parts will be warmer than toast. Then the fun begins. If both of you are aroused and ready when you reach the bed (you might hand him some erotic literature to read while he waits, just to be sure; and of course, a little self-pleasuring while in the tub should bring you where you want to be), he can enter you right away. The contrasts in body temperatures provide a stimulation which simply must be experienced. It can't be described. If you want to add to it even more, bring along a cool washcloth to wrap around his penis for a moment or two before he puts it in. Give it a whirl. I think both of you will be pleasurably surprised.

For sheer sensory pleasure, few experiences can match the lover's bath. But talk about sad ironies. In a culture which is obsessed with a chrome, plastic, and detergent cleanliness, we aren't raised with a sex education in bathing. So many fun things can be done in a bath or shower, this ignorance approaches a male-female tragedy. I haven't even begun to talk of all the things the two of you can do in a tub together. Sure, one of you has to sit with your back to the faucets (unless you're sitting on his "lap," which gets down to something a bit more basic), but that's a small enough price to pay for some memorable hours together. For one thing, the tub is a great place for conversation, provided, of course, it isn't serious conversation. (Who would ever want to talk about the European Common Market while you're playing nice naughty games with your toes under water?) The tub is a fabulous place to share your sex fantasies, a sort of "You tell me your raunchy thoughts; I'll tell you mine." It's also a great place for dining. If you haven't tried it, do yourself a favor. If you can get hold of one of those makeup trays which fit across the tub, they work fine. Or you may be able to build one without much fuss. But if nothing else, you can always set a TV tray alongside the tub and enjoy some hot hors d'oeuvres and cold wine while you and your man soak together. With the occasional addition of warm water, you can turn a deep bath for two into a seven-course banquet.

Under the warm, deep waters, a glass of wine, a bar of soap, and thou: Pure ecstasy!

8

The Second Most Relaxing Thing You Can Give Him

You now have him out of that tub or shower and you have patted him dry with a thick, man-sized, towel (patted, not rubbed). What can you now do in the way of pleasuring that man of yours? No, not that, unless he's really insistent. That can come later. Loving is like a candy cane. It's more fun when you prolong the enjoyment.

And what could you add at this point? Right! A massage. A genuine, honest-to-god massage has to rank among the top half dozen great gifts one human being can give another. And what could be more truly human? Have you ever seen one chimpanzee give another a massage? And for dogs, cats, and lizards, it wouldn't even be possible. But you and I can become expert at giving, and at times receiving, this delightfully human gift. It is the ultimate in sensuous ministering. Show me the man who won't go for a full-body massage and I'll show you a man suffering from a severe sunburn!

In the past few years we have seen massage parlors spring up in the cities like mushrooms after a spring rain. And sure I know most of them are not legitimate massage parlors, or let's say they offer something more than muscle-kneading, but the fact is massage has become recognized as well worth the pursuit of the modern male. And, in the name of equality, the modern female. Encounter groups, sensitivity sessions, and others interested in turning-on to sensory awareness (translation: doing what feels good) have taken up massage with a passion. We can now find a number of books on massage at any bookstore, and many of them have some positively stimulating ideas. On the other hand, some of that "stroking the forearm with a feather" business isn't likely to turn on any man—unless he's a fetishist of some sort. So what I'm going to talk about are tried and proven methods of giving a man-pleasuring massage as only a woman can administer it.

First of all, get rid of any ideas you may have about the necessity of possessing a set of bulging biceps in order to do the job well. Massage is something like judo. Learn the correct techniques, and you don't need a lot of muscles. The secret is in your hands and what you do with them. And potentially, that's a lot.

I suppose you could give your man a massage anywhere in any position, even standing up. You could, but not well. When he returns from those workaday battles and collapses in his chair with a scotch on the rocks, you might massage his neck and shoulders, but it's so very limiting. Not only is there too little of his body to work on, he can't get satisfactorily loose, and you can't use your hands the way you should. If you're going to give him a massage worthy of the name, you have to get him lying down and as relaxed as possible. If you can afford to go all out, I think a portable massage table would be the ultimate Valentine gift. Without a massage table, you'll just have to look around like the rest of us and make do with what is available. The idea is to find a flat, firm (but not uncomfortable) surface, one high enough that you can easily work on him while standing without having to bend over. A dining room table padded with a couple of blankets and a pillow might serve well. If you use the floor, you'll still have to bend over while on your knees, but then, sometimes that has something to say for it: You can straddle him and get good leverage in your arms. (Besides, with both of you nude, it feels nice.)

When you're planning a loving evening, try to have everything ready beforehand. Interruptions while one or the other of you search for this or that is like pausing during the final movement of a symphony while the first violinist looks for his bow. Whatever you may employ, lotion, oil, rubbing alcohol, talcum powder, vibrators, or anything else your imagination and his preferences may dictate, have them ready and waiting when you begin. If you give one another massages in bed (which isn't the best place to massage but does offer other advantages), you can keep your "supplies" always on hand in the night stand.

Now that everything's ready, down to the fun! You can, of course, give him a massage without any lotion or oil or anything, but unless you have run out of everything, I can't think of any reason to. A little lotion goes a loving, long way. My preference, and that of my man, is for a body oil. There are a number of them now on the market. I think most are over-priced. But you can mix some up yourself for next to nothing. Pick up a bottle of safflower oil at your supermarket. Yes, that's right, the same polyunsaturated oil you use for cooking (but not corn oil; it's too thick). To about four cups of safflower oil, add an ounce of essence, whatever scent turns you and your man on. You can buy essences of just about every exotic aroma from sandalwood to seaweed (jasmine is a favorite of mine) in an import specialty shop or a place which sells psychedelia—incense, black-light posters, etc.

Get him to lie down on his tummy, arms down by his sides. Of course, you can begin on just about any part of that body of his (excepting the most exciting parts, unless you want the excitement to begin and end before the massage), but for the sake of convention, let's assume you start at his shoulders. Pour the oil or lotion on your hands, not over him. If you pour it over him, it can run all over the place, and it can also be chilly; your hands warm it. Work the muscles across his shoulders and down his arms and shoulders in a way which will leave him limp all over. The idea is to give him a massage, not just a stroking with lotion. Use both hands, and use the muscles in those hands and arms of yours. And spend time; lots of time. If there is one thing besides love-making and gourmet dining which shouldn't be hurried, it's massage.

I'll let you in on a pet theory of mine: Sexuality can be conveyed through the hands. If you think sexy and feel sexy, you will communicate it in the way you touch him. I don't know how this happens, and it isn't one of those things Masters and Johnson have wired people for and collected data on, but I'm absolutely sure that when I'm feeling deliciously raunchy, my man is going to know it through my fingers (and *not* just when I'm touching him *there*). Try it. I guarantee it. While you are moving your hands over him, think of all the wonderful sexy experiences you've had and the far-out fantasies you've dreamed of. If you're astride him while you give the massage, he is bound to feel your moistness against his back, and what could be more of a turn-on for him than that?

As your hands move down his back (or up his legs, depending upon where you start), you can set off some special fireworks for him if you learn where his erogenous buttons are and what to do to trigger them.

Men *do* have erogenous areas on their body which include more than the genitals, despite the fact that most sex manuals ignore them. They may not be as erotically sensitive as some spots on a woman's body, but they do exist, and a smart gal can learn to make good use of them. The small of the back and parts south is a good one. I've heard it has something to do with a bunch of nerve endings concentrated in the lower part of his back, but whatever it is, it's there. Most men can be turned on by feminine fingers to their back below the belt line. I don't mean just giving him a muscle rub like he might get at the athletic club. That's all right if he has been bent over digging postholes all day and feels like he has been stretched on a rack, but otherwise, think of your all-important goals. You want to leave him feeling mellow. Tranquilized. And maybe with just the beginnings of sexy thoughts. Why only the beginnings? Remember, you don't want to turn either a bath or a massage into a sexual demand. If you go about it in ways which tell him all you are interested in is getting his male organ erect enough to service your panting passions, you may not find him accepting the next offer. O.K., if it's already very obvious he wants to score and can hardly wait, you can move right along from the bath and/or massage to the feminine art of sexual loving. But until you're sure, don't turn a massage into a demand.

Move your fingers in circles and figures from his waist to his buttocks. You can move the palms of your hands over the same area. With your hands well-coated with oil, you can give sensations which are pure cloud-floating.

When you get your hands on his buttocks, you can have lots of fun. A lot of men may not know we gals are turned on by a foxy male fanny, but we know, don't we? And with him all nice and relaxed, those muscles are such fun to play with. They move so deliciously under your fingers. They're like a couple of water-filled balloons. You can move them all around and make them quiver in such a delightful way. The gal who doesn't get all sorts of wonderful warm feelings skillfully playing feelies with her lover's fanny, hasn't yet discovered the joys of sensualism (or you can read that *womanhood*). But hey! Don't get carried away. If you get too playful with your fingers between his buttocks, you are getting into some very primary erogenous areas and your massage is likely to turn into a fast sex scene and the leisurely loving will be over. If you want to really relax a man, I've found three massage areas to be most responsive. The neck and shoulders, of course. That's where we all feel the tightness when we've just slugged our way through one of those manic-depressive days. I have a hunch women could cut the ulcer and coronary rate in men down to nothing if they practiced giving their men an after-work-neck-and-across-the-shoulders massage each day. And what they would do for masculine virility might be the nicest thing to happen to women since cavemen started dragging home cavemates. The second area is the low back and buttocks. No gal has to be told how good that feels, does she? Certainly not if she has ever gone through the last three months of a pregnancy. It's been said that humans were never meant to walk upright and that walking and standing around on two legs rather than on all fours is the cause of our aching backs. Add to that sitting all day at a desk and you have the makings of a tired bottom. You get it, and so does he. Your magic fingers can take the feelings of fatigued fanny completely out of your man. And it's wildly sexy! Third, there are his legs.

I have a pet suspicion, one of many. I think the current ideas of what is sexy in the male is a creation of males, not females. We are forever being told we are turned-on by men who are tall and broad-shouldered. Nobody ever says anything about the way trim hips and marvelously male legs can make a girl follow a guy down the beach. But we know, don't we, that for every "leg and ass" man, there's a "leg and ass" gal. I don't know for sure whether my man has aching legs when he gets home from his stint at the office, but I'll give his calves and thighs a slow, lazy massage just in case. No one can accuse me of a shortage of self-interest!

When you go to massage his legs, be sure his knees are bent. If you don't, the most you'll be able to do is rub his skin; the muscles will be too taut to massage. One of my favorite ways to work on his legs, especially his calves is with me sitting or kneeling back on my haunches with his knee between my legs (he's lying on his tummy). This way he can have one knee bent and relaxed, laying it up against my front and shoulder. (I kind of dig rubbing my cheek against his foot. Is that strange? Who cares?) With his leg relaxed, you can work those muscles in his calves like warm putty. You can move those muscles up and down and from side to side freely. And there's something about hairy male legs which make them so very touchable! But when you come to those thighs of his, watch it! I hate to be repetitive, but you and I have to remember his erogenous responsiveness. You know what the stroking of your inner thighs will do to you. Well, he has feelings too, and that includes the inner thighs. If you play around too long, or too high, from his knees to his balls, you can count on a rise in response, but for your sake, play it cool; take your time. A massage should be a massage. It *should* be a massage. Honest! Don't get threatening by getting your hands into places where the massage becomes obvious. You can get a much greater pay-off if you give that massage to "unwind" him. The minute you start getting "grabby" and try to push those buttons, you may find him turning down your offer of a massage, and then where does that leave you?

After you have worked on him from top to toe on his backside, you can start on the other side. The front side, I find, is often sadly neglected. Most gals don't know what to do with it except those things which should only be left until later. Fact is, a frontal massage can turn your man into as much melted butter as a job on his shoulders and back. Lying on his back, you can sometimes get more effective leverage working on his neck and shoulder muscles, especially when you are kneeling astride him. It's about the only way you can properly massage those neck muscles which tie up with tenseness. (Besides, straddling him is always fun, isn't it?) He also has pectoral muscles on his chest which can be massaged. Those are the muscles gals develop when they want to expand their bustline. The exercises don't grow breasts; they just push out what you have. Massaging his breast muscles can even be an erotic experience for him. While men may not have nipples which are as sexually sensitive as a woman's, some men can definitely be turned-on by having their nipples properly stimulated. Plus, if he has put in a day painting the kitchen ceiling or hanging wallpaper in the guest bedroom, those pectoral muscles are going to be as sore as his back. Rubbing them with the palm of your hand may not work wonders, but it can't do any harm, and it does add to your total touching experience. Which is also the reason why I think it's great to massage his abdomen. I know the books on massage don't include chapters on tummy massaging, but I don't have any ambitions to be a masseuse. I just want to make my man feel as good as he makes me feel.

And I found it feels good when he massages my tummy so when I have the chance, I return the favor.

Theme and Variations: Some of the "massage" parlors in California and New York advertise in the underground press that they offer Danish, French, Japanese, Spanish, Finnish, and Italian massage. The first time I saw such an ad, I thought, "Wow! Maybe I can pick up a lot of new ideas to try out on my lover." I called one of the places with the view in mind of buying an hour or two of instruction in these foreign techniques. And what a shady used-car operation I discovered behind those tantalizing claims. All a "French" massage amounted to was the "services"—whatever they amount to—of a gal with a name like Fifi LaRue. The "Japanese" massage was administered by an oriental gal, and, well, you get their gimmick. I don't know; maybe some men have a nationality fetish. In any case, I didn't learn anything new. But then, they were honest enough to not take my tuition money.

I have, however, learned one thing: There isn't a thing any massage parlor can offer our men that *we* can't top. At a legitimate place, they can get a good professional massage which is great if they suffer from competition in a twenty-mile bike race. But there won't be much that's sensual in it, and sex in such establishments is a definite no-no. The other places offer even less. Some gal wearing a toga or bra and panties takes a few swipes at the customer with some rubbing alcohol or talcum powder. She collects ten dollars for that little routine, then she bargains for her sexual services, and you can bet they run more than the "massage." Every once in a while, the vice squad raids one of these places. Personally, I think the consumer advocates ought to investigate them! Twenty dollars for a three-minute hand job. Outrageous!

As for gimmicks and special techniques of massage described in some of the sensitivity session awareness books on the art, I'm largely unimpressed. I can't imagine a man being turned on by being stroked with a feather duster or plastered with a mud pack. At least not any I know. They strike me as similar to

those cute recipes you read in the women's magazines, the ones
for rutabaga soufflé and clever hors d'oeuvres of one-inch crack-
ers spread with carrot-flavored yogurt. I don't know whether
they are concocted for *any* members of the human race, but the
gal who would serve them to her man is asking to end up spending her evenings at a lonely table. One such psychedelic,
pseudo-oriental massage book had a whole chapter on working
on his back by walking up and down on it in your barefeet. If I
tried that, I'd probably slip and break my neck—as well as
fracture his back. And are my feet on his spine really going to
give him a thrill? Unless he's a masochist? I also find myself
turned-off, and I mean totally, by the entire body-touching
mystique of these "sensory awareness" advocates. They make
a big thing of massage and touching, feeling, and "relating." It's
all supposed to be oh-so-good for my psyche, my self-discovery,
and my ability to understand my fellow man. Well, they
haven't sold me. As far as I'm concerned, my fellow man will
just have to struggle along without relatedness and feelies. If
some other man's woman isn't giving him the touching he
craves, I'm sorry for him, but there is only one man's body I
want my hands on, and it is only his hands I want roaming
over this body of mine.

I've found a few variations, however, which can give my man
some extra pleasuring from time to time. First has to be the em-
ployment of a good vibrator. A hand vibrator should be as much
a part of a sensuous woman's boudoir equipment as a vanity
mirror and a douche bag. (Honesty compels me to say the
purchase of a vibrator isn't a bit unselfish. There are only two
or three things which feel better to a woman than a thorough
massage with a vibrator, and ever since "J" wrote *The Sensuous Woman*, every gal knows the things she can do on a leisurely afternoon with a vibrator while she waits for her lover to
come home. If you don't yet know, good grief, girl, pick up a
vibrator and start a program of self-pleasuring; you're missing
out on the best of all answers to what to do on a lazy afternoon.)
When you buy a vibrator, get a good one. There is very little

difference in price between the cheapest and the best, but there is a tremendous difference in satisfaction. Buy one of those heavy-duty models the barbers use, the kind which strap on the back of your hands and allow you to turn each of your fingers into high-quality instruments of something indescribably sensual. Some of those "fully illustrated" sex books now on the market—you know, the kind you may not learn much from but are fun to browse through together during an evening before the fireplace—suggest ways you can pleasure your man with one of those phallic-shaped "personal" vibrators. With one exception which I'll talk about in the chapters to follow, I don't think these vibrators have much to offer in man-pleasuring. They just are not constructed for it. They're built for a woman. But with the conventional heavy-duty vibrator, you can do all sorts of incredible things to him and for him. I've never had the chance to experience giving or receiving this one, but I think just about the ultimate in everything we can do for each other would be a massage with a vibrator on each hand. Can you imagine all that tingling going all over you? Wow!

On an excessively warm summer evening, the love-making urges of your man may be dampened. He comes home with a wilted shirt and a wiped-out constitution, ready for nothing but a cold drink and a quick collapse. His head may hold amorous thoughts, but with the temperature and humidity something close to a sauna, he's left limp in more ways than one. O.K., it may not be your night for sex either, but there is still something very nice you can do for him—and, for that matter, he can do for you: an alcohol rub. For this, of course, you need a bottle of rubbing alcohol, and rubbing alcohol has that hospital odor which is less than a turn-on to many. Well, there is probably no way you can kill that odor altogether, but you can mask it somewhat by lighting some incense in the bedroom before you start.

Pour some rubbing alcohol into a pan or bowl and drop a washcloth or hand towel into it. The time-honored nursing technique of the alcohol rub is to pour the stuff over you straight out of the bottle. Personally, I think it leaves something to be desired. It runs all over the place, and it can have a sort of shock effect which isn't much fun when you're all in the mood to relax. With a washcloth, you can control the flow of alcohol over his skin. I like to lightly squeeze the excess out as I take it from the pan, then lay it out across his shoulders and draw it down over his back. It isn't really a back rub or a massage. When I move my hands over his moistened body, it's more a caress than a rub. If I really want to cool his hot skin and refresh him all over, I straddle him and fan him after I've put on the alcohol. Alcohol evaporates quickly and that does the trick, which is the secret of aftershave lotions. After he is cooled by alcohol, you can finish it off with a light caressing with talcum powder. There are now some really great exotic scents on the market which won't leave him smelling like Mother's cologne. Oh! One word of caution when you use rubbing alcohol on him: Alcohol can sting, so be careful of any knicks or scratches he may have, and keep it away from his genitals and between his buttocks.

One last suggestion for something very nice you can give your man by way of massage: a foot massage. Even if he hasn't been selling vacuum cleaners door-to-door all day, can he possibly fail to appreciate something which feels that good? Could you? Even if you don't have the chance to make it an all-over massage, a foot massage can do wonders in taking his kinks out. Your skilled fingers with some skin lotion, preceded or followed by a warm-water foot bath, can open the door to a lot of returned loving. And let me suggest a variation you might like to try: a foot massage with table salt. With his feet wet, pour out a palmful of salt and give each foot a vigorous two-handed massage. There is nothing quite like it for leaving feet feeling alive and well refreshed. Just be sure he hasn't any scratches or blisters; rubbing salt into wounds is not your intent. And needless to say, wash the salt off afterward.

Someday, some wise philosophers and scientists will get together to explain why a massage does so much for one's psyche as well as one's body. But until that time, we will just have to suppress our curiosity and accept what wonderful things it can do. It spells the difference between a good wife and a great mistress, a gal who is satisfying and one who is superbly sensual. Show me a gal who makes a point of giving her man a lover's massage at each opportunity, and I'll show you a woman who gets more than her share of pleasuring in return. And isn't that what it's all about?

9
Erotic Games I

For anyone looking for examples of sexual inequality, I have the all-time worst robbery since the U. S. Army stole the land from the Indians. It's those sex manuals which include a chapter on that heating-up of the female called *foreplay*. They're enough to make any woman who likes men and the great sexual things which can be done with a man want to burn books. They all take that same stupid tack: A woman is supposed to be two-thirds frigid by nature; a man doesn't need any sexual loving to get him turned-on and ready; therefore, it is up to the guy to do all sorts of things to his gal to raise her passions to the pleasure point. And if he doesn't stroke, tickle, and otherwise titillate her into a frenzy before he gets down to the final thrusts, she won't catch the brass ring of the elusive orgasm. And he will be a loser in the league of lovers. And what is she supposed to be doing while all this is going on? Why nothing, of course. True to that timeworn "The man is aggressive and the woman is passive" dictum, these silly sexologists don't give the gal anything to do but lie back and enjoy it. I'm surprised more men don't approach loving as a servicing task to be performed, and women as little more than selfish bitches.

Well I'm willing to lead a crusade to work for very total equality when it comes to pleasuring your partner in love. That's why I've thrown out the word *foreplay* and coined the word *twoplay*.

Twoplay recognizes what you and I know: that any normal gal likes pleasuring her man every bit as much as she enjoys being pleasured by him, and that all those delightful sex games are meant for two, not just one. Furthermore, twoplay gives a gal the opportunity to play all sorts of red chips to get more of everything she wants from her man.

Before we get down to the business of specifics in a gal's twoplay techniques, let's pause to consider some basic principles of the art. First, often ignored, is an understanding that not all twoplay is aimed with sex as the goal. In fact, truly great twoplay may go on for an entire afternoon and/or evening without orgasmic sex for either of you even intended. Then if it happens, fine, but if it doesn't, well that's great too. No demands on either side. Second, all twoplay should communicate. If it doesn't talk to him in the words you want him to hear, it just isn't going to have the effect you desire. You do, after all, want to practice the art of loving, not just sensory exploration. And just what should it communicate? That's easy. It should tell him he turns on his woman and that she *is* his woman. It should tell him what you want him to know: that his body is what you want—what you *need*— to make you come fully *alive!* It should communicate that he is your very desirable man, and that you love him. Love him! Love him!

Let's talk about loving, then, for just a minute or two. With everything that's been written about, talked about, and sung about love, one would think none of us would be in any way confused about it. But we are. In fact, we are so confused, many of us feel *love* can't possibly be defined. Yet that doesn't stop us from saying, "I love (undefined) you," and "I want to be loved (undefined) by you." Maybe there should be a rule: If you don't know what love is, don't talk about it; you just make matters worse!

Having laid down the rule, I will now wrap myself in a cloak of arrogance and authority and state that I feel I do know what love is and what it means between a man and a woman. My definition: *Love means valuing a person.* Feeling that he loves me means feeling that he values me, everything that I am, intellectually, emotionally, physically, that he places me high (hopefully, even at the top) of his list of priorities, that my feelings, thoughts, and responses are important to him. He loves me by letting me know by his words and actions that I'm a *person,* a very special, desirable *person.* How much of this is sexual? All of it, if you go along with me in thinking of sex as something much broader and all inclusive than just what we do with our genitals. He is a man; I am a woman. When he takes my hand in his, when he laughs at my jokes, when he glances down at my cleavage, when he lights my cigarette, when he turns down the sheets on my side of the bed, when he kisses my shoulders and tells me I smell nice, when he listens—really listens—to my opinions, likes, and dislikes, when he lets me know he is turned on by the sound of my voice, the touch of my hair, that new recipe I try out on him, and my views on moon shots and macrame, then he is responding to me, a woman—his woman. And there is a lot which is very sexual in it. No one of my sex can make me feel like that. And when it comes to what he can do for me physically, well there is literally nothing which can make me feel more important, more needed, and more cherished.

Loving him means trying in all the big and little ways to affirm his manhood, his importance to me. Many years ago I learned what every woman with an interest in the other sex learns: that the most important thing to a man is to feel he is *needed* by his woman. But unless I'm a total incompetent, he knows I don't need him to make my decisions for me, pay my room and board, or guide me through a revolving door. I like being a "kept" woman. It's great—with the right man. But I don't *need* it. No real man wants a dependent, helpless, pathetically stupid little girl. Regardless of what the strident lib crowd may say, the average man is not so hungup with inadequacy feelings and so easily threatened that he can only feel comfortable with the dumb little house mouse. To mix my metaphorical species, the house mouse is an albatross around a man's neck, and the average guy chokes on it. He wants me capable and self-assured, but at the same time he wants to know I need him. And the biggest way that comes through for him, and for most men, is in my *sexual need* for him. In one hour of his love-making, he can make me feel every inch a woman; he can make me feel alive; he can make life very much worth living. And am I going to let him know I need him for this? In every way I can think of!

The best way I can think of, and absolutely no exceptions, is in the ways *I* make love to *him*. The feminine games of twoplay tell a man how much he is needed by his woman. And his response is going to give her everything she needs. We've already talked about bathing him, massaging him, and understanding his male sexual dreams. Now he's all relaxed and aroused. You can start making love to him in earnest.

A man with an erection is a beautiful sight. Any woman who doesn't agree has problems—severe ones. There is something so *assertive* in that male organ in a state of arousal. Maybe it is the wonderful awesomeness of it which has given so many gals the idea that once a man has attained an erection, he has reached the peak of his sexual arousal and he doesn't need or desire any more stimulation. They climb between the sheets with their man and expect him to do all sorts of wild erotic things to them to get them in a mood of intense eagerness. Since they discover an erect male organ greeting them when they cuddle up, however, they don't put in any effort to bring him where they want *him* to bring *them*. It shortchanges the poor guy and, in the long run, the gal is apt to get less than she wants from the sex session. He has erogenous areas you can do things to with your hands and other parts of your body just as you have. And if you don't take advantage of them, look out! Some other gal just might.

Every skilled call girl has learned to use her hands to a sexual-turn-on advantage. And every gal who wants to drive her man out of his mind with the right kind of desires will learn to do the same. I've always suspected what those Hawaiian gals meant when they said, "Keep your eyes on the hands." There are a lot of things you can do to him with your hands, and he'll love all of them.

Let's start with a few words about the male sexual anatomy. You no doubt know a lot about it from firsthand experience, but we can all stand a review from time to time. The penis is a truly amazing organ. It can double its size, almost double its diameter, and go from soft as putty to hard as rock. And all within the span of a few thoughts. It is an amazing phenomenon, one I never tire of observing. As I said before, for reasons having to do with that phallic ego in men, most guys take pride in their organ when it is erect, but are insecure about it, maybe even a little embarrassed, when it is limp. If his gal makes a pass and he doesn't have an instant erection, he feels he has let her down, or failed in his masculinity. What's worse, some women I've talked with expect that instant-erection response every time they drop their chemise. And if it doesn't happen, they feel rejected. It's the sort of sex-on-demand attitude guaranteed to turn most men impotent. And with men in short supply, who wants to do that? No gal should expect a man over sixteen to get an erection every time she flashes some flesh at him. Guys are not robots with quick reaction buttons. We like our men to do things to us to raise our passions. Why shouldn't we expect they will want the same?

Unless the guy is just too beat for any loving (or it's too soon after his last climax), a clever gal can start with him limp and bring him to a delightfully demanding erection. The key to it is to not make it demanding. In some of those plotless sex films (the ones where the couple always seem to be glancing sideways at the camera), the male actors have real problems keeping it erect. Why not? What man could perform under lights, camera, and the critical eyes of who knows how many? The actress then invariably goes to work to get him back in a state to do what the director wants him to do. And she does it in the worst way. She grabs his penis and starts vigorously jerking on it as if she were a contestant in a milking contest. They go at it as if they were trying to whip a dead horse back to life. I actually think it's more fun to start your twoplay when he's soft. Most of the times it is erect when you're playing those wonderful games, so the novelty of something "different" in your hands is itself a sort of turn-on.

But don't start your twoplay at that all important organ, soft or firm. There is no rule says you can't of course, but half the fun of erotic loving is in the build-up, and the more you put into the build-up, the higher the rockets will soar for both of you when they finally fire off. I like the inside of his thighs as a warm-up. Stroking, with just the fingertips, all the way from his knees, and feeling his muscles tense with desire for me to go further provides a sense of woman-power which does great things for my female hormones. Don't get me wrong; I'm not trying to torture him. When men refer to a girl as a "prick teaser," this sort of twoplay isn't what they mean. They mean a little bitch who dangles the bait but has no intention of ever coming through with any complete loving. My man can enjoy the suspense because he knows I'm not going to slam any doors: I'm just as eager as he is. A man's thighs may not be as erogenous as a woman's, but the message in your fingertips which says, "I dig touching your body and my hands are getting closer all the time to where you want them to be," is bound to give him good feelings.

There are times when I enjoy having him do nice things to me while I play my games with him. Other times, however, I like taking over and pleasuring him while he just lies back and imagines he is an Eastern potentate being served by his favorite harem girl (at least that's my fantasy). Talk him into letting you take charge next time. You can stretch out the loving to a point beyond a woman's wildest dreams. It turns your ultimate orgasm into a monumental experience, the kind a woman remembers and takes out of her file of memories to brighten a dull Monday morning or a weekend when he's out of town.

His penis becomes erect when some erotic messages from his brain trigger a response which fills the erectile tissue with blood. (It is the same mechanism which causes our clitoris to become erect and swells up, engorges, our labia.) If you place a couple of fingers between his legs directly behind his scrotum as he is getting an erection, you can discover something interesting: That's where his erection starts; and that is where the muscles which contract when he ejaculates are located. What is important to our sex, however, is not the male anatomy, per se, but what we can do with it, and that area between his balls and his anus is decidedly erogenous in most men. Try stroking it and pressing your knuckles against it (not *too* hard). It is also a spot which is sensitive (in the right way) to temperature in a way some men find exciting (applied, of course, with sensitivity). A warm washcloth, wrung almost dry, and not too hot, pressed tightly up between his legs under his scrotum while you do other things to him with your free hand is one possibility. Another is a suggestion I read in a "marriage manual" several years ago (I can't remember the title or author; a British writer, I believe): Have your champagne ice bucket or a dish of crushed ice beside the bed. As your man is just about to climax, press a small handful of crushed ice firmly against him there. According to that sex authority, it's supposed to trigger a response in him like nothing else. Great, that is! It is one suggestion I can't recommend personally. My man doesn't even like the swimming pool when the water temperature drops below that of a lukewarm bath. But then, it might do great things for your guy. You can always try it and hope it doesn't give him pneumonia or send him crashing through your mirrored ceiling. There is one thing he isn't likely to object to in the slightest: Massage up and down on that spot with the vibrator on your hand. If you have a personal (phallic) vibrator, you might try pressing it against the spot. Frankly, however, I don't find they give as much stimulating vibration.

Stimulating his scrotum and testicles can be a great kick for both of you, but as every gal knows, "Handle with Care" is the word. I think most men are just a little skittish when a gal starts playing with that pair of cute things hanging in that sack between their male legs. From the reaction of most, getting kicked in the balls must be the stuff of which male nightmares are made. This doesn't mean you have to keep your hands off, however. They're toys which are too much fun to leave alone. Cup them in your hand and lift them up against him; then move them in nice loving circles. With some body oil on your hands, those little spheres inside that soft little bag move under your fingers in a way which makes any woman feel like laughing and panting at the same time. And judging from reactions, men find the experience more elevating than sky diving. When we do things with their penises, either with our hands or our lips, they get a plus, from what they say, when a soft female hand caresses that pair of male glands which makes it all happen. And so very well!

Now to that primary organ of his: Whether you call it a penis, prick, cock, tool, or whatever (ever notice how many aggressive names we give it?), you must admit it is the nicest thing God ever created for the benefit of women. I must admit I can never in any way understand when some woman says she doesn't like to touch her man "there." How can a woman keep her hands off anything which makes her feel so great? I not only want my hands on it I want to be able to do things to it which will make it eager to do things to me! And I'm sure you feel the same.

Men vary in the way they enjoy being handled, but every man (weirdos excepted) enjoys a versatile woman's hand on his most sensitive, versatile organ. Since most guys are gallant enough to say they like everything loving their women do, it isn't always easy to find out what has the greatest effect. It's largely trial and error. We can all develop our manual techniques faster and to a better level, however, if we stay aware of how that marvelous male anatomy works where sex is concerned. The head of the penis is the sensitive part. Not that the shaft is insensitive. Get careless with your fingernails and you'll soon find out. But the head is the most sexually sensitive spot on a man's body—by far. You already know well what his male organ looks like and feels like, but there are a couple of important details of it which are worth talking about. That little rim which circles the base of the head is called the *corona*. Have you noticed it is covered on the underside with kind of rough little bumps. They add to our pleasure when he is plunging in and out. While the entire head is literally loaded with nerve endings, it is around the corona that his penis is most responsive. There and on the underside of the penis at the little strip of skin which "attaches" the head to the shaft. If you haven't taken the opportunity for a close inspection lately, do yourself a favor. As the little girl said to the little boy she found relieving himself in the bushes, "That's a handy thing to bring on a picnic." Some years later, I'm sure she found out how handy it was for other things as well. It is truly a fascinating piece of anatomy. And while you are inspecting, try a few things; discover what will best bring him what you want him to have, feelings that no other woman, anywhere, can turn him on so well. Use your fingers well, and you can have him in the palm of your hand. (I know. Bad pun.)

Make sure your hands are lubricated, at least lightly, with lotion or body oil when you play games with his penis. As you know, his skin there is soft and easily irritated, but just as important, he will like the feel more. Now try this: Grasp his organ firmly with one hand. Press the palm of your other hand against the head (remember, well-lubricated) and make the sort of movements you might if you were polishing a brass doorknob. If thirty seconds of that doesn't have him ready to do all sorts of wonderful unspeakable things to you, run him in for a physical checkup; he may have a burned out bearing or two. Of course, there is a drawback. You can't keep this sort of stimulation up for very long. If you do, you know what will happen: Whoops! And it's all over for him for a while. Only a guy with a lot of control (or very limited preliminary games) could take over thirty seconds of it without the rockets exploding. Now of course, there may be times when that is the objective of both of you, but we'll talk about that later.

Another little trick that's lots of fun for both of you. Place your fingers around the head as you might if you were going to unscrew the cap from you favorite bottle of cologne and make gentle, but firm, unscrewing movements around the corona. With just the right amount of pressure in your fingertips, and his reaction will tell you how much is "right," you can enjoy the satisfaction of some great male reactions. The best of woman power! Whether it's sensitivity, dexterity, or superior tactual imagination, we can do superior things to our partners with our nimble fingers. And I don't care if someone calls me a female chauvinist! Another fingertip technique you might try, for example, is to place the fingertips of both hands around the base of his penis and slowly draw them up toward the head. I think it's the anticipation as much as anything which makes it good for him. Anyway, what the heck, it's fun for us, isn't it? And don't we have a right to play with our favorite toy at least half the time?

A couple of things you can do to him which are designed for more, shall we say, intensity: Take his penis between your palms. Press palms together and roll the penis back and forth as if you were rolling dough. So long as your palms are well-oiled, you can use as much pressure as you like. It'll drive him out of his head—and he'll love you for it. The other technique is probably the thing you did the very first time you got your hand on one of those awesome male organs. Remember? He probably put your hand around it and moved it rather vigorously up and down in the way most guys masturbate. It may have been the only way he reached a climax with you during those days in the front seat of his car. If you want him to "come" in a hurry, it is about as effective a way as any. But golly, he can do that for himself. You can provide something better than that. Much better. Nevertheless, let's admit the method still has something to be said for it or so many guys wouldn't spend so many lonely hours with it. The idea is to not go at it so vigorously. Grip it firmly just behind the corona. And when I say firmly, I mean *tight*. If your hand is well-lotioned you don't have to worry about gripping it too tight. (Remember those porno novels? They always make a point of how "tight" the heroine is.) Your hand will slide with the lubrication without making him feel like you're skinning him raw. Move your hand up and down over the head slowly. And I do mean *slowly*. So many of our sex complain that men don't take enough time, we certainly don't want to be guilty of any quick, one-two-three, ready-set-go approaches. And when we are using this maneuver, it will all be over all too soon if we do!

How long can you keep up doing things with your hands? Unless he is unusually keyed-up or has some problems with control, just about as long as both of you might like. The secret is in cooling it down when he lets you know he is reaching the point of no return. And when I say cooling it down, I mean *stop*—at once. Another couple of moves may be too much. If you then take your hand away for about a minute, the intensity should subside and you can return to the pleasuring. By taking such a breather every once in a while, you can prolong the loving to your heart's content, and let your own sensual feelings build to just where you like them. And of course, there is nothing says he can't be doing things to you with *his* hands while you're doing your thing.

There may be times when you would like to bring each other to climax with your hands alone or with your lips and hands. Some of the old sex book writers used to call it "mutual masturbation" and it was a decided no-no. They were the same old prudes who advocated the missionary position with the lights out as the only "normal" way to engage in "conjugal relations." I've often thought their wives (if they had any) should have been awarded masochism medals for tolerating bedroom boredom. "Mutual masturbation," however, 'is a contradiction in terms. Masturbation is something you do to yourself, not to and for your lover. Your man may find it a turn-on to watch you masturbate; a lot of guys do; and you may wish to entertain him this way from time to time, but for now we are talking about you bringing him to climax this way. There are times for all of us when intercourse is either out of the question (due to illness, menstrual cramps, or that no-sex period following delivery) or just not desirable. Your man may feel slightly wiped out after a hard days run in the handicap. Thoughts of things carnal may still be in his mind but coitus, let's face it, takes some up-beat energy, especially for a man, and regardless of which position you select. So why not offer those oh-so-soft feminine hands of yours? You can't play red chips much better. It's also something nice you can do for him when time is short, say when he has only ten minutes before leaving for the office. Or when the two of you don't have the greatest privacy; remember those evenings at a drive-in theater or sailing in a little open boat. (But please, for safety's sake, don't practice your manual art where one gal said she does: while her man drives the fast lane on the freeway!)

Incidentally, one way some couples practice hand-loving beneficially: Let's say it's late afternoon, they're feeling so sexy they can hardly keep their hands off one another, but friends are due for cocktails in an hour. They might, of course, peel off their clothes, have a romp, and put themselves back together before company rings the doorbell. But she might not care to have her hair mussed and her false eyelashes unstuck with only minutes to spare. And both of them might be looking forward to a long, long evening of lots of loving. A real full session in the afternoon could cut down on the chances, but a little loving by hand wouldn't take much zest out of either one of them. In fact, it might even help him go longer in the evening. Some guys who have control problems find it helps if they masturbate a few hours before love-making. Even without any other reasons, however, it, like the other sex games the two of you invent, can be a lot of fun. And it can give you ten more points on his scorecard of *The Most All-Woman Woman*.

Oral sex is a variety of loving which has gotten much more attention than anything either of you do with your hands. Maybe that's because the sexologists are still trying to convince the inhibited that they can do it without losing their morals, their minds, or their teeth. Perhaps there is sound reason behind their campaign. Not until the Kinsey reports hit print in the late forties did anybody admit to anybody that they were doing what just about everybody else was doing in the bedroom and that a lot of it had to do with lips, mouths, and tongues. Matter of fact, oral sex is still against the law in California, and maybe elsewhere. So we are talking about a law which has been violated more often than prohibition. Kind of adds to the excitement, doesn't it? All right, even if it doesn't, I still find it an interesting comment on our society for whatever it's worth.

Just about every book on sex of the past twenty years has included a section on oral sex, but I think a few things more need to be said. For one thing, few of them say anything about *how-to-do-it*. And that's what we all need to know, isn't it?

We can do just about as much for a man with our lips, tongue, and mouth as we can with any other parts of our female anatomy. Which is why men are so turned-on by the whole idea. That isn't to imply they can't do equally great things to us in a similar way. We know they can. But men often have a particularly strong thing for it. So why shouldn't we develop our expertise?

Putting a man's sexual organ in our mouth might have been the last thing in the world we would have considered—before, that is, we fell in love with a particular man. Then for most of us, a lot of attitudes changed, and oral sex was one of them. We found there wasn't anything dirty or unclean about it. And after a short while, we learned to like it—a lot. Now let's see if we can make an art of it.

You might first give some thought to the position he (as well as you) may assume when you begin. It isn't the question of the ages or anything, but like all loving, it's an art which is worthy of some serious forethought. On a strictly physical level, any one of several positions may be equally satisfying. When it comes to things sexual, however, more goes on in our heads than in our genitals, or at least as much. Some positions for sex are psychologically more a turn-on than others. When the two of you are going to make the oral sex mutual, you don't have a lot of choice as to positions. Unless you're contortionists and have imaginations which go far beyond mine, it comes down to lying in reversed positions, head to toe, the so-called "69" (think of the figures 6 and 9 and the man and woman). He might lie on his back with you above him or kneeling over him; you could lie on your back with him above; or you can lie on your sides. And that's about it. But since we are talking about techniques for pleasuring him (and cashing in on a lot of woman-pleasuring in return), let's consider the best position in which to get him when you want to take charge and show him what you can do to drive him gratefully out of his senses. You can ask him to stretch out on his back while you sit on the bed and bend over him. Nothing wrong with it as far as what you can do for him, but how long can you bend over like that without getting a crick in your neck? And it would be a shame, wouldn't it, to have to break off just when things are going great guns? Persuading him to sit in a chair while you sit on the floor between his feet is not only more comfortable for a woman, it may have a good effect on his male psychology, his phallic ego. It has elements of that "harem girl serving her master" that fits his fantasies. The same applies when you have him stand while you kneel before him to make oral love, but maybe you should suggest he lean back against something. When you really turn it on, he may get weak in the knees. Of course, the equality-obsessed feminists would see it as subservient and "demeaning" to "serve" a man on their knees, but none of them has ever been well-pleasured by a man. If I find a thousand-dollar bill laying in the street, will I get down on my knees to pick it up? Damn right! And what he has to offer me is worth a lot more than a thousand dollars. A thousand dollars has never given me an orgasm.

Using her mouth to make love to a man offers some decided psychological advantages to a woman. I'm sure you know what I mean. The word is *power*. Every sensuous woman enjoys to the fullest (i.e., to the most arousing) using her skills to drive that tiger of hers to a frenzy. It's a real turn-on to bring him up to a peak in a way nothing else can. I can play that "passive female" role and let him do all the loving, but if I do, I'll shoot down my own self-esteem; I won't have anything more going for me than I would if I were a rubber mannequin outfitted with the necessary artificial equipment. With a talented tongue, I can get him just where I want him—wanting *me!*

When making oral love to a man, there should be one cardinal rule: *never hurry.* He may want you to take it in your mouth, as much as possible and as deep as possible, right from the start. Ordinarily, a woman can best make love to her man by taking her cues from him; he knows best what will pleasure him. But here I think we have the right to do it our way and in our time. And we can linger all we like. We hold the reins. For openers, I think it's fun to think of it as one of those giant Christmas peppermint candysticks. You want to make it last as long as you can, so you don't devour it. I don't. I unwrap several inches of it and slowly lick the whole length of it all the way to the top. Of course, I have to hold it around the wrapped end, but that still leaves a lot of candystick to lick. Every millimeter your tongue moves up that male organ of his builds his pleasure anticipation higher. Sure, he can hardly wait for you to reach the head. That's where most of those sexual nerve endings are. But you're in command, remember. Don't linger when you get there. You can do plenty of that later. It's your candystick; enjoy it. A lot of members of our sex who don't have to worry about calories have discovered how much fun they can have with a can of whipped topping. It can be licked off with a tantalizing slowness. I suppose chocolate syrup, honey, or strawberry jam might also add variety, but I don't know how one would handle all the stickiness. I'll stick to whipped cream. And if you can't afford the calories? Don't think about it. You can skimp on lunch the next day.

While you are letting your tongue roam around, don't neglect his scrotum and its contents. His woman's tongue moving over and around his balls is a high, high turn-on to any woman-loving male. Some of those technical sex writers will tell you different. They'll say he doesn't have those erotic nerve endings or whatever they call it there. But they are the same jerks who say the same thing about the vagina, that it doesn't have the nerve endings in it and that a woman's entire kicks comes from the clitoris. They may know their anatomy; but they don't know sex. You might try taking one of his balls into your mouth and running your tongue over it like you might with a lollipop. I can almost guarantee he'll love it, but watch it. Don't forget, that's his most vulnerable appendage. A little too much pressure, and you may give him pain rather than passion.

In what may be the most highly publicized—and truly hilarious—porno movie to date, *Deep Throat*, the gal who is cast in the lead is found to have a most unusual physical problem: Her clitoris is located in her *throat!* This, explains her doctor, is why she has found conventional sex less than satisfying. It also makes the remedy obvious to her: deep-throat oral sex. Impossible? Not at all, as she proves for the camera, and no trick shots here. Why not? If a sword swallower can take a twelve-inch blade down the same passage, surely any one of us can take everything our man has to offer. Heck! the star of *Deep Throat* sure can, right down to his pubic hair, and I'm not willing to take second seat in man-pleasuring to anyone. And I don't have to. And neither do you. Most of us had the feeling at first of being shocked when he thrust it in too far. Maybe even a gagging sensation. If you know what I mean, you also know it's a real downer. You experience a momentary anxiety, and you may feel more than a little nervous when you attempt to continue.

Since a gal with a "deep throat" is the fantasy of most men I've talked with, it might be to our advantage to learn the technique. And it can be learned. For the most part, it comes down to learning how to relax. Easier said than done, you say? Well, maybe. The key to the whole thing is for the woman to take over the action—totally. If the man is on top thrusting in and out of her mouth as if it were her vagina, he will strike the back of her throat and trigger a reflex gagging. And that fear of choking will simply add to it. He has to be persuaded to let you do it all. Get him to lie on his back without moving. Then, with you over him, you can lower your mouth at your own pace and gradually relax enough to take him much deeper. It also helps if you are in a position to keep your head tilted back (just like the sword swallowers do). Can you breathe while you're doing it? I doubt it. Even the very talented star of *Deep Throat*, Miss Linda Love, has said she has to hold her breath and occasionally come up for air. But that's no problem. A lot of us have learned to swim the length of a pool under water. A quick breath, and you can go back to a technique of man-pleasuring which will convince your man you are truly one in a million.

Sometimes you may want to go all the way and bring him to climax with your mouth. Great! What you can do with your hands, you can do with your mouth—for the same reason and with the same advantages. Plus something more: Just about every man gets a big ego boost having his woman make him "come" with her lips and tongue. As one guy was honest enough to admit: "It makes me feel twenty feet tall, a real super stud." The first time, however, I think every woman faces the same minor hangup: What to do when he comes? I had one pretty sophisticated gal tell me, "I really dig sucking on that thing of his, but I always keep thinking, 'What if he can't keep control and he comes in my mouth?'" She hadn't thought it out, but she had the idea such a thing could only lead to some dreadful consequences. Understandable? Sure. For whatever reason, myths and fears about this have cropped up like crab grass in suburbia. To answer just a few of them in one sentence: No, semen won't rot your teeth, give you heartburn, or result in pregnancy. In sufficient quantity, it might cause you to count calories if you were on a ridiculously rigid diet (although I'm told it is mostly protein), but even if you're making love to a superman, there isn't much more than a tablespoon of it, and that won't add any inches to your waistline—not even if you make it daily. And in case you are still wondering about it: We are likely to get or give more germs *kissing* than we are in enjoying oral sex.

For any reader who may not know, it has a slightly salty, not at all unpleasant, taste which some women say makes their mouth a little dry. Some are neutral; others enjoy the taste. Maybe it's like avocados or caviar: an acquired taste.

From what I've listened to, however, what bothers women

more is a feeling of being drowned, or, as one cute little blonde put it, "The first time it happened, I felt like I had my mouth over a fire hose nozzle when somebody turned on the hydrant." We all know what she means, don't we? When that climax occurs, it's like WHAMO! He explodes! I don't know the pressure per square inch, or the shooting distance, but I do know it can feel like a warm, liquid rocket going off in your mouth. Quite a surprise if you don't feel it coming.

Fortunately, there is a physical tip-off. When he reaches the trigger point, you can feel it. The contractions of those ejaculatory muscles begin just before. When they start, if you place your tongue right near the little opening in the head, you won't get that jet stream against the back of your throat. And you won't have to suddenly pull away as if the whole business turns you off. After all, none of us wants to risk making our man feel rejected.

Once you've taken everything he has to offer, what then? I recall what one writer had to say of his first experience in being pleasured by mouth. She was a prostitute he picked up in a bar in North Africa. She did a great job he said, but as soon as he climaxed, she scurried over to the sink and began vigorously spitting. He felt totally wiped out by the whole routine. Little wonder. It's like saying, "I find you repulsive." Fortunately, it didn't sour him on oral love. He said he later found out not all women react that way. If she doesn't want to swallow it, she can dispose of it subtly in a handkerchief without a production of spitting. Actually, since it doesn't taste bad at all, I can find no reason for spitting it out at all. And I can find one very big reason for swallowing it: him. One husband told me what happened when his wife finally decided to go all out in her loving. "She told me she was going to give me the damnedest blow job I'd ever had, and believe me she wasn't kidding. It was unbelievable. The greatest! I said, 'Did you swallow it?' She kind of laughed and said, 'of course!' Well, you know, right then I felt like a king, like she wanted to be my woman in every sense of the word. Wow!" I don't know whether you could call it a male ego trip or what. I don't much care. Anything which can get that kind of a response has just got to have some fabulous pay-offs for his woman. And that's enough for this gal.

After you have tried all those fun games with whipped cream and chocolate syrup (variations which have now become almost old hat—but still fun), here are a couple more you might experiment with:

If you are drinking a chilled wine, hold some in your mouth for a few moments before going back to making love with your mouth. The idea is to chill your mouth and tongue, so even an ice cube in your mouth will work fine. The sudden change in temperature can give him an added lift. Try it; you'll see. And for my other suggestion? One that is designed for laughing and loving fun. Encircle his penis with your lips right at the base of the head (behind the corona). Then, *hum*. Honest, I'm serious. Humming produces an effect a little like a vibrator. What you do with your tongue while humming "The Battle Hymn of the Republic" is up to you. And his musical tastes. It's a great technique for couples who tend to take sex too seriously.

Another suggestion for twoplay: anal stimulation. In a man, as well as a woman, the anus is highly erogenous, but something, probably taboos or niceties, kept it a big secret. Never a word in those quaint old marriage manuals that used to stress how gentle the husband should be on the wedding night in order to keep his frightened little bride from suffering a lifelong trauma. But this is today, and we can open up our heads, remove any taboos and silly ideas, and drop in a few more ways to turn-on our men. If you decide to start with a massage, and you know he is in the mood for a full session of loving sex, what would be more natural than to let your fingers slide between his buttocks? *Teasing* is the name of the game—at least at the start. Run a fingertip around his anus, around that little ring of sphincter muscle. Tease him with the thought that you may go a little further and you'll find yourself with one very randy and ready male. What he wants, of course, is for you to insert your finger, but as with all love-making, the teasing builds the tension. The longer you prolong your games of twoplay, the greater your own turn-on as well.

While we can be aroused by anal stimulation as much as men can, and maybe even more so, the reasons might be different. When she feels his finger inserted in her, she is undoubtedly going to feel some stimulation in the vagina. The two orifices are separated by only a thin membrane. And why wouldn't that feel good? Our men have something else. Less than a finger length up his anus and to the front he has a prostate gland which has a lot to do with his sexual functioning (a good enough reason why it should be important to *us*). When you have him over on his back and you're doing delightful things to him with your mouth, you can slip your finger up there and stimulate that gland. It's almost certain to virtually double some already mighty strong male responses. Just enough prostate stimulation alone is enough to bring most men to ejaculation—or at least close to it. Among all the other gadgets provided us by modern technology, one can now purchase a battery-operated anal stimulator, one of those personal vibrators with a soft plastic fingerlike attachment. If you're one who likes having the latest in bedroom appliances, you might be the first on your block with this one. On the other hand, you might be the last. The others may have beaten you to it.

In case you haven't noticed, in this chapter as well as the last one and the one before that, there hasn't been a word about what he may be doing while you are treating him to all these goodies. Well just in case there is any question, I am not leaving all the loving to women. My man loves me very thoroughly and very well, and I have no intention of discouraging him. But no one can convince me I'm not entitled to equal rights when it comes to loving. If he can pleasure me, I can return it—and maybe even do him one better. At least I'll be in there pitching. For any sensuous woman, it's the greatest turn-on of all.

10
Erotic Games II

Want to read descriptions of 57 positions for sexual intercourse? I didn't think so. I've read those *variety-is-the-spice-of-your-sex-life* books too, and to tell the truth I find those descriptions so mind-boggling I can't keep my mind on sex. I'm frustrated trying to remember whose leg is "to the outside, flexed at the knee, at a forty-five-degree angle" to something or other, and whether "supine" means I'm lying on my back, on my tummy, or riding his shoulders. By comparison, I can decipher a foot-ball-play diagram with ease, but then in football, I know what the objective is; in these sex-by-the-numbers books, I don't know whether the aim is to discover how many ways two anatomies can bend, to prove the creative imagination of the writer, or to provide couples with a new puzzle to be solved every night for two months.

I have nothing against variety in positions. Quite the contrary. I've tried it up, down, sideways, sitting, kneeling, standing, and a few other ways which defy description, and I can't say I've tried a position I didn't enjoy. They all offer something. It depends mostly on his mood, and mine, at the time. And on where and when we make love. If we do it in the back seat of the car, we obviously don't try it standing up. And if our love-making is in the shower, we'd be creased, mutilated, and spin-dled trying it in the missionary position. But variety? It's great!

I suppose, however, someone might still ask, "Why all the emphasis on variety; isn't sex in the good old-fashioned *wife-on-her-back-with-legs-spread-and-the-husband-on-top* good enough?" A fair question. After all, if it was good enough for Grandma, why shouldn't it be good enough for us? One excellent reason I can think of: Grandma probably got more kicks from a sewing bee than a romp in the bedroom. It was good enough because she and Grandpa never tried anything better. The painful fact, and I think we all hate to admit it, is that sex can be a *big fat bore*. The words stick in my throat. It's awful to have to say anything bad about something so good, but I also love thick steaks, very dry martinis, and football, yet I couldn't face steak and martinis three times a day, and by the third televised football game New Year's Day I can't tell you who is playing. Do *anything* over and over again in the same way and I don't care how good it is; it will tend to get boring. Even sex. This is one reason I'm a strong advocate of sex in different locales—a living room floor before the fireplace, bending over the kitchen table, in the swimming pool, on a beach, in a hammock, a sleeping bag for two, or a sauna. I haven't yet tried it astride him on horseback, but I have plans. Some positions offer more visual stimulation than others. Some provide more body contact. Some positions are great when we feel in a very active mood, others are best for times of leisurely sex. If I'm feeling lazy we can do it in a way in which he can pleasure both of us without much energy on my part. (Not that I stay passive; at a time like that, I couldn't lie there like a corpse even if I tried.) When he's had a full day of driving to some vacation spot, I can return the favor. He can take it easy, stretch out on his back, while I climb astride and provide the greatest relaxer ever discovered. There is another reason for varying positions which may or may not have importance to a man but can hardly be overlooked by a woman: When the position is changed, his penis enters from a different angle. If he enters from the front, he "hits" the back wall of my vagina. From the rear, it is the front wall which receives the most intense stimulation. When I'm astride, I can rock-to-and-fro and feel it all the way to the hilt, and it can make my hilt feel positively delicious. There are also a couple of positions with the two of us almost at right angles to each other which are great for variety—and sensations. (The only drawback: We can't touch as much of each other.) Those 57-different-positions sex manuals always try to list the advantages and disadvantages of each position. This always strikes me as dumb. If a position has any disadvantages, surely the two lovers will discover them. Is there some special need to be forewarned? After all, if my man and I decide to shift to a different position, who says we can't? On one of those adventuresome evenings, the positions will equal my orgasms, and we all know we have a numerical advantage over men in that department.

I'm still not going to try describing all those various positions. I'd probably just get things confused and then somebody might try them and end up with a whiplash injury or a dislocated hip. But there is another, more important, reason: This is a book for sensuous, mature women. And while any woman with a healthy sex drive and the right man wants to improve her art of man-pleasuring, she doesn't want to play "sex instructor," which, of course, is what might happen if she strolls into the love nest with her book of play diagrams under her arm. Our men are not morons. They all know it can be done face to face, or from behind, the man on top, or the woman on top, sitting, standing, kneeling, or lying down. When I'm in the mood for one position or another, I let him know, but I'm sure I don't have to discover any new ones for him. And if your man has a woman who is the sort of intelligent free spirit who would be reading these pages, he just has to be the sort of imaginative, uninhibited lover who comes up with all such discoveries by trial and error (with very few errors). So having dispensed with numbers one through fifty-seven, what is left to be said about what the sexologists call "coitus" (and most of us have a more fun word for it)? Plenty!

First, and perhaps most important for a woman, is the question of *when*. And God knows I don't mean any of that "I'm too tired tonight" or "I just don't feel comfortable doing it in the afternoon" or "You mean you want it *again* this week (month, year)?" If they ever pass a "Never on Sunday" rule, I'll vote for dropping Sundays. I'm talking about that critical moment when all the things you've done to each other with hands, lips, and whatever else you've thought of have brought you to the point where there is only one thing which will satisfy that deep-down craving. Can there be a man-loving woman who doesn't know what I mean? No matter what he may have done with his fingers, mouth, vibrator, or fertile imagination, or how many times he may have brought me to an orgasm by any or all such means, there comes a point at which all I want is that first thrust of his penis in me all the way to the hilt. But I'm sure I don't have to tell *you*. Every woman with the right head, the right equipment, and the right man knows there is simply no sub-stitute. We women vary, however, in our rate of "heating up." Some of us are ready in about eight seconds flat, give or take a couple of seconds; others get going a little slower, or even a lot slower. (But one thing I know: Those old purveyors of folklore who contend women are as slow to respond as an obese eunuch have never taken a real woman to a motel for an hour, or do you suppose those characters have some special talent for turn-ing off women?) There is one, however, we all know: We can't simply lie back like Cleopatra on her barge and wait to be pleasured to a purple passion. Without the proper erotic state of mind and maybe even a little self-stimulation before coming together with her man, a normal woman, but one of the slow responders, will have a rough time getting her motor operating at sufficient speed to set off her rockets.

No matter how well a man knows a woman and her telltale responses, he can't know when she has reached that hair-trigger point when she's ready to be sent into orbit. He can't read minds, and he can't read what's going on between her thighs. I've listened to a lot of members of our sex complain about their men not taking enough time; the guys are all through before the women are anywhere near an orgasm. These

frustrated wives read an article or two about premature ejaculation, and they're ready to pack their men off to see Masters and
Johnson. If all such women were lined up in rows, they would
make the hordes of Genghis Khan look the size of a scout troop.
I am certainly not going to say the problem doesn't exist. It does.
There are some men who climax even before they enter, and
for others it may be no more than one or two thrusts. But I have
talked to women who wouldn't be close to orgasm after twenty
minutes of vigorous thrusting (that is if they could find a man
capable of such a highly controlled performance). And I'm sure
all of us know by now that the best time to have a man make
that first fabulous thrust is when we are right at the brink of
orgasm. Then those first few strong thrusts can make it happen.
If he goes on from there, great! Who would turn down the
chance of it happening again? Which all means that it is up to
the woman to say "Now!" to her man when she has reached her
readiness point. Of course, if he is already in position and you
have his penis in your hand, you won't have to say anything;
just put it where you want it. And what about those times
when he just can't wait and you would like a little more time?
O.K., so your timing can't be perfect every time. Just don't
treat it like a big overwhelming frustration. His climax, like
yours, is a reflex reaction. He isn't rejecting you or punishing
you when he comes; he's responding to you. And tomorrow is
always another day for more practice on the timing. Anyway,
that myth about simultaneous orgasms being the only great ones
has been dead for ages. Let's face it, we can reach orgasm before, during, or after his, and it can happen for us more than
once. So why should we ever get out of shape over something
which doesn't need to take away our satisfaction in the least?

When we reach this point in sex, it seems to me the mechanics
are quite simple. We are down to the basics, just a demanding
penis and an eager vagina. Those walnut brains who say a
woman's feeling are all in her clitoris have never interviewed
most of the women I've talked with. And surely don't speak for
me. Anyway, I think those old "clitoral *vs.* vagina orgasm"

arguments are silly, and I'll bet you do too. Whatever feels good, feels good. Right? Who needs to analyze? It comes down to the simple, basic, marvelous matter of a male organ moving in, out, and a few other ways in a female organ.

Except maybe even anything so basic can be improved. Or at least enjoyed to its fullest potential—yours and his. Until Masters and Johnson turned their research curiosity toward the matter, we didn't know much of what goes on in these female bodies of ours during sex. Now we know. And it's fascinating. They very effectively disproved many notions which had been kicking around the marriage manual literature for decades. For one thing, they showed women are just about as quick to respond sexually as men. The telltale feminine response, secretion of vaginal lubrication, occurs about as quickly as a man achieves an erection. They also found most of it comes not from the Bartholin gland, as every sex book used to state, but from the lining of the vagina itself. Some of those old marriage guides routinely advised the wife to use K-Y jelly or some other such lubricant, on the assumption, I guess, that the bride isn't going to be turned-on, that she is just naturally frigid. What a sad view of women! Some women don't have sufficient secretion, especially as they get older, despite their arousal, but for the average gal, a couple of erotic thoughts is enough to create some very wet panties.

They learned a few other things which are even more important to us. Right inside the entrance of the vagina, something fascinating happens when a woman is fully aroused: a tumescence occurs which works to tighten the entrance. It makes for a tighter fit around his penis. This part of the vagina is called the "orgasmic platform." Of course, some of us discovered this, and a few other things, from personal exploration, but it was satisfying to know the researchers were finally able to explain the whole thing in scientific terms. They also found that when a woman reaches the point where orgasm is imminent, the inner end of the vagina sort of balloons out and the uterus is pulled slowly back and up. This distention of the vagina swells out the inner two-thirds to about twice the usual size and it lengthens about 25 per cent. What all this means is that when she is fully aroused, and he is in her all the way to the hilt, her vagina is actually going to grip the *head* on his penis *less* than it might if she were not at all aroused. On the other hand, the tightening in the outer one-third of the vagina is greater. At orgasm a number of contractions occur in this orgasmic platform—up to 10 to 15 times. The duration and strength of the contractions varies from woman to woman and from one orgasm to the next. As just about every experienced gal knows, that squeezing sensation is something which earns rave reviews from men. Those contractions at orgasm are, of course, involuntary. They're part of the whole reflex reaction of a female climax. But the muscles in there can be brought under feminine control. And that can be a huge advantage for us as well as them. Some of the erotic books from the Orient describe the talents of expert courtesans who have developed those muscles to an Olympic-gold-medal-winning degree. Personally, I think the descriptions of "milking" a man dry and dizzy are a little overdrawn, but the potential is there and it can be developed. There was even one company (I don't know if they are still doing business) which manufactured a device to aid in training the muscles. I've never seen one of the gadgets, but from the description it sounds a little like one of those carnival devices where for a penny a guy could register the strength of his grip on a meter (proof of masculinity number 179). I have enough appliances filling my nightstand drawer without sending off for one of those, to be delivered, of course, in a plain brown wrapper. Plus the fact that it can be accomplished without it. Any gal can practice on her own, in the afternoon, for example, when you've finished your before-he-comes-home bath.

The muscles are associated with the same ones, or the same muscle group, as the anal sphincter. When you tighten that anal muscle, you also tighten that other muscle, at least to a degree. That isn't all there is to it, however. Unless we had a most unusual upbringing, we weren't taught anything about those vaginal muscles and what we can do with them. Chances are, we were not even aware of their existence. We might be contracting without even knowing it. Or we might think we are tightening up when we are not. So first we have to get acquainted with them. Insert your first and second fingers in your vagina (one finger isn't going to be enough; they won't contract *that* much). Now start experimenting. Tighten the anal sphincter and the muscles in your buttocks. As you try various things, you'll hit upon what works and you will be able to feel the squeezing on your fingers. It's simply a matter of body awareness. When we were infants, we had to discover what made our fingers work and what made our toes wiggle. It's pretty much the same thing. Once you discover how to contract those muscles, you can set to work building them up. None of us may ever get to the point where we can lift weights with those muscles, but I know from experience they can be employed for something a lot more fun. And incidentally, they can also be used to give both of you a lot of pleasure while at the same time delaying his climax. No, I don't mean that you squeeze it off. It works like this: If a man goes at it vigorously, plunging in and out, he is going to come before either of you could count to one hundred by fives. Which is great, of course, if that is what both of you want right then. But if you want to draw it out for a while, the fast, all-the-way-in-and-all-the-way-out, movement isn't going to make it. If you can persuade him to put it all the way in and keep it right there while you squeeze him with that trained muscle of yours, you can stretch things out while providing some very exciting sensations for both of you.

Regardless of what position the two of you try, no man wants a woman who remains "passive." If he does, he could do as well with a mannequin or a corpse, and if you have a guy like that, run, don't walk, right out the door. Regardless of what anyone says, a man wants his woman as a sex partner, not a sex object. Objects don't *initiate* it; they don't even *participate* in it; they just *submit* to it. The woman who is actively in love with her man is active in her loving. In the woman-astride position, almost all the action is hers. She is strictly in control and can speed things up or slow them down as she chooses, which is probably why it is so appealing to many women. Other gals have some hangups about it. They feel it reverses the roles making the woman "dominant." And some men feel the same. I say it's ridiculous. When he's on top, I don't feel dominated; I just feel pleasured. And when I'm on top I never feel I have snatched his manhood away. For any position, a woman should learn how to move most effectively. All it takes is a little practice. First, by yourself, then with him. If you ride a bike or swim much, you may have developed some good thigh and calf muscles. You're ahead of the game. It's those muscles, plus the buttock muscles, which we use the most, although the back muscles and even those in the arms and shoulders can be brought into play.

Some of the old-style strip-tease dancers had the movements down to perfection in their bumps and grinds (and I always secretly envied the ones who could hang a tassle from each nipple and make them twirl in opposite directions like twin-engine propellers). Talk about ball bearings in their hips! No topless go-go dancer could even compete in the same league. For practice, stand with your toes three or four inches from the wall. Swing your hips forward so that your pubic mound presses against the wall, but don't touch the wall with any other part of you. Go up on your toes and with only your pubis make circular movements on the wall a little like you might if you were trying to polish the spot. If your man walks in, you can tell him you're trying to rub out a stain. Make the circles as wide as possible. And yes, I know. When you first try it, you can really feel a pull on those back and leg muscles. Most of us don't get much practice arching our back except in bed, but that, after all, is what we are practicing for. That rotating movement, what the strippers call a grind, can turn sex from something great to something fantastic. Ask him. On second thought, you won't have to. You'll know. You don't use the movement when he is making those deep in and out strokes. If you were to try it, you could have a slight slip in co-ordinating your movements which might hurt.

If he has ever hit the "wrong spot" in one of his thrusts, you know what I mean. When you *can* employ the grind to the maximum is when you persuade him to put his penis in all the way and hold it there. (Grip his buttocks and press him hard against you to be sure he doesn't begin any pulling and pushing.) As you rotate around on him, you'll find he is stimulating you way down deep in places you had forgotten you had, and doing things for him which marks you as an expert lover. Don't expect, however, to become accomplished at this arched-back hip rotation in one or two trials. Moving the hips in a circle with your bottom sticking out is easy unless you suffer from rheumatism. But doing it with your back arched takes some practice and maybe the build-up of some muscles. A gymnast could probably do it easily, but if you are like me, well, I had trouble getting a passing grade in P.E.

The other big movement to develop is, as you already know, that to-and-fro, forward-backward movement. It's obvious. So obvious that most women I have talked with thought of it as something like a reflex movement, a little like a knee jerk. And I can easily understand why. When he starts those wonderful plunging movements, it would be close to impossible to hold back and not meet him movement for movement. But "doin' what comes natur'lly" may not do everything you want it to do. If you were making it with a male mannequin, you would have no problem. The dummy wouldn't be moving back. But a real live man is almost certain to be contributing a lot of action of his own, and if those movements don't mesh with yours, it can be something like a car motor that keeps missing: It gets you where you're going, but the ride isn't as much fun. I'll see if I can describe what I mean by synchronized movement. Imagine you have two balls, each attached to a string. You hold the end of the string between your fingers, one in each hand, far enough apart that you can swing the two balls toward each other and have them touch as the pendulums swing all the way, but not so that they crash. The two pendulums, of course, are the hips of the two of you, and the motion should be a free-swinging movement, not something resembling a pair of colliding rams. The bumps the strippers throw at their audience may provide a visual turn-on, but if a gal threw her pelvis that hard in bed, both she and her lover would end up battered and bruised. It's like a fist slamming into a wall. And while I'll grant you that sometimes hard-pounding action makes for a great, wild, finale, that pendulum synchronized swing provides a sensual oneness that is everything love should be.

Most of us were taught to walk, sit, and in other ways move like ladies. It pleased Mother, the dean of girls, and nervous fathers. But along the way, we may have forgotten how to move like women. We may have developed that welded-in-a-ramrod-straight, immovable-hips style of making love as well as walking. It's easy to spot. Watch the hips of women you pass on the street. Most walk with a locked pelvis and a jarring flat-footedness. All right for a Marine walking his post on guard duty, but feminine it is not. When we were kids, we used to hear about "loose" women. Do you suppose it had something to do with their freedom of pelvic movement? If so, I'm all for becoming a loose woman. There is an exercise which is fun. It's part physical and part frame of mind. First, think of your pelvis as a basketball swinging freely from a string attached about your waist. That's the key to it: keep the picture of that swinging ball in your head. You want to complete an arc forward and back with your tethered basketball. As the method actors would say, "You have to close your eyes and *see* your pelvis as free, free, *free!*" To get it swinging, walk on the balls of your feet. Stay off your heels. And keep your legs together. To start, and keep, the ball swinging, you need a slight up-and-down bounce on the balls of your feet. You can feel it when the swing is right. Remember, you're not trying for that side-to-side fanny swishing à la Mae West in this movement. The swing is front-to-back. You won't want to try this in the same exaggerated fashion on the street. You'd feel like a damn fool (although you might get a lot of male attention, if that's what you're looking for). But while you are moving around the house or apartment, waiting for him and having delicious thoughts of anticipation, you can get in plenty of practice. Personally, I think any and all exercises are best done in the nude if for no other reason than that it adds to the body awareness, earthy feelings, or, what the heck, just because it feels good. Anyway, be sure you do the exercise without shoes. Otherwise, your ball won't swing.

Next, take your swing to bed. By yourself—this is just practice, remember. If you have a water bed, you have at least a 100 per cent advantage to start. On an aquatic mattress you can undulate like a playful dolphin. I don't know what the inventor of the water bed had in mind, but he came up with the nicest thing for women since the vibrator. Even with a 250-pound man on top, a water bed permits a gal plenty of swinging room, and with none of that pinned-down feeling. But conventional mattress, water bed, or living room floor, the exercise is essentially the same. Lie on your back with legs extended and together. To get the swing here, you have to arch your pelvis up with pressure across your shoulders and on the back of your heels. It may seem like quite a lift when you first try it, but with regular exercise, you can swing it a good foot off the mattress. Then if you can talk him into not laying all his weight on you when he's on top, but instead putting his weight on his toes and elbows, you can treat him to an incomparable experience. When your timing is just right, nothing—and I mean absolutely *nothing* —plumbs the depths of a woman's sensuality quite as much, so as always, there is a selfish motive, but you can be sure you will hear no complaint from *him*. An active woman can press all his response buttons. And that's the sneaky aim in the whole thing, isn't it? A little expert pleasuring brings a whole heap of pleasuring in return. And Wow! It's so good!

When you reach the top of your swing, contract those buttock and anal muscles of yours. It not only tightens those all-important muscles under that vaginal platform, it gives an extra push upward to receive him. And it increases the sensations for you. And here, let me give you another suggestion: with him on top, and after he has entered, bring your legs together. This will, of course, put his legs outside both of yours. Not only will it give you a firmer "grip" on him, it will allow you greater leverage in lifting up. And every little bit helps. This will all depend, of course, on his feelings and preferences. The aim, after all, is pleasuring him as well as yourself, and with his legs outside yours, the penetration isn't as deep. Anyway, you can always change around.

Lastly, learn to use your leg muscles. If it is only for sex, and not for six-day-bike racing, you shouldn't have to build them up through exercising; just the amount of walking you do should have them in good shape. Those 57-different-positions sex books always include the one in which the man is on top and the gal lifts her legs high enough to place them on the guy's shoulders, but that doesn't take leg muscles, just a very flexible back. Personally, I see only one redeeming feature in it: very deep penetration, if that's your thing. It doesn't allow much activity on the part of the woman; about all you can do is hang on and hope you don't come out of it wearing a back brace. You can get the advantages of the position, however, without the spine-stretching drawback if you wrap your legs around him (with him on top, of course). In wrestling, I think they call it the scissors hold. But there is a difference. You don't want to squeeze him around the waist. He might turn blue, rupture something, or belt you in the ear. Wrap your legs around his hips, locking your feet at the ankles. The trick, then, is in co-ordinating your leg movements with his thrusts. With your ankles locked, your heel should be between his buttocks. The idea is not to lock him in a vice. If you grip him between your thighs too tightly, he won't be able to get much swing in his pelvis, and what a loss that would be. You open your thighs and relax your knees as he pulls out, then when he thrusts, you pull your calves up, pressing your heel in against his buttocks, pushing him into you in the same way you might if you gripped his buttocks with your hands. It not only adds an extra measure of good feelings physically for both of you, it communicates an "I want you, all of you" message. It's a technique which takes a bit of practice, and the practice has to be done with him participating. It's all in the timing. Practicing with a pillow between your thighs won't do it. It may take a few tries to get the timing down just right, but I'm sure your man won't object to the practice sessions. Especially when he feels the results.

Are there times when a woman is not active? Not unless the position makes it virtually impossible. In a rear-entry position with you on your knees, there isn't much you can move around unless it is a small side-to-side movement while he holds all the way in, and in that position, with your legs hooked over his shoulders, I don't see how you can move much of anything but your hands. Other than that, sex for a woman is a very active sport. At least for a woman who wants the most from it, and one who digs the satisfaction of becoming a certified expert in man-pleasuring.

I've got to say one more word about female action. It isn't really action, I suppose, but you can call it what you will. It's those sounds you may or may not make during sex. Have you ever watched a good porno movie? The gals moan, groan, and scream while they're biting the bedsheets. Are they for real? I don't know. I doubt it. But maybe the producers are tapping some very real male need. I don't think groans, screams, and yelps have any erotic turn-on value in themselves, but we all know we want some feedback from our sexual partner. A woman has the advantage. When the man reaches orgasm, the gal *knows* it. She doesn't have to worry if "it happened for him." There is no sure way for a man to be sure what, if anything, is going off within her. Hence that question which is so annoying to so many women: "Hey, baby?" "Uhm?" "Did it happen for you?" "Did what happen for me?" "Did you come?" "Uhmmmm!" I don't think any of us like feeling we are having our pulse and passion temperature taken—pass/fail. And we have all heard it said these inquisitions represent male insecurity. Maybe so, but so what? Analysis doesn't work to stop him. Tell him he is insecure and you won't help your own cause. You may just increase the insecurity. But insecure or not, he still likes to know what you are feeling is good, very good, fantastic! So, should a nice girl from a small town in the Midwest cast her inhibitions aside and let loose with the sounds of the jungle? So long as it doesn't scare the horses or send the populace to the air-raid shelters, why not? The moral mothers of the PTA wouldn't approve, but we all know their problem, don't we? I'm not saying you have to moan and scream or that you ought to carry on with amorous sounds when it would mean nothing more than it does with the actresses in the porno films. But if you do feel like moaning or screaming or laughing, by all means, let go. Do it! You may want to think twice if doing so is going to scare the mood out of him or wake up your mother-in-law asleep in the next room. (You can always bury your head in the pillow to muffle it.) And if vocal expressions aren't your style, even if you've rid yourself of those silly old inhibitions, don't worry about it. There are other ways to let him know your reactions. You can tell him. Next to "I love you," the nicest words which can be said about sex are, "Thank you; that was the *greatest!*"

11
Bedtime Laughs and Conversation

Show me a lover with a sense of humor and I'll show you a lover that *is*. Richard Burton had it all together when he said, "If you can't laugh together in bed, the chances are you are incompatible anyway. I'd rather hear a girl laugh well than try to turn me on with long, soulful secret looks. If you can laugh with a woman, everything else falls in place."

If there are two things couples don't do about sex, it's talk about it and laugh about it. At least that's my conclusion after talking to quite a few. They may say a few things about it when and if it turns into a pitcher of sour cream and they head for the courtroom. Too bad. Erotic pillow talk is one of the best preventative medicines a couple can take for their relationship. Besides, it can be a whole lot of fun. And if that isn't reason enough, what is? As for laughter, well, when you're happy, don't you feel like laughing?

I don't like to think of hangups. There are enough problems in the world of personal relationships—everything from feminine hygiene to generation gaposis. Who needs to talk about more? But I guess we have to admit men and women have one hellish old time talking to one another. And nowhere more than in sex. I've talked with couples who have never once talked over their love life in twenty years of marriage. Some of them seem to feel it's a moral no-no. I remember reading one of those anything-fun-must-be-a-sin marriage books not many years ago in which the pathetic puritan author said the only time husband and wife can "licitly" discuss their "conjugal relations" is when it is necessary to the successful completion of the act! I guess that's when they don't know when and where to put what! But to talk about sex for the fun of it, or to get more fun out of it? Never, never, never! Such couples will batter each other with boredom talking about kids, unpaid bills, unrewarding jobs, and inclement weather, but they'll wrap their genitals in a chastity belt of silence.

I don't think Kinsey has any figures on it, but it is my impression men have more of a problem talking about sex than we do. And wouldn't we expect them to? They have their masculinity to prove. And they are still the ones expected to be the aggressors and the teachers when it comes to sex—according to our sex-stereotyping society. So naturally, if a guy isn't sure he has all the answers, all the techniques, or all the self-assurance and freedom from inhibitions, he just may want to avoid sticking his neck out in a free-wheeling rap session. A smart woman can, nevertheless, open up the most reluctant of lovers.

First, there is the matter of what words to use. And what ones maybe not to use too much. Words can gum up our conversations so darn much it's a wonder we communicate at all. At times, I feel everybody speaks a foreign language. We all inhabit our Tower of Babel. He reacts one way to certain words; you react differently. And when it comes to sex words, boy, do the differences get in our way. There is one school of thought which holds that since our sexual acts and sexual parts all have "scientifically correct" names, we can solve sexual-communication problems easily by simply using these "right" words. Maybe so if we are going to talk about sex only in a scientific way. Which is fine for Masters and Johnson and your gynecologist, but terribly dull in the bedroom. Furthermore, those words make sex sound so depressingly clinical, like something out of those TV medical dramas. I don't want to "engage in precoital stimulation"; I want to play sex games with my man. I guess that enrolls me in the other school of thought, the one which sub-scribes to the use of those other words, the ones they bleep off the talk shows. They have two advantages: They seem a lot more natural (after all, I'm not a physiologist), and they have a greater turn-on value. And if you are going to talk about sex, why not make it as natural and as arousing as possible?

Well, it isn't always that easy. Words like *cunt, prick, fuck, tit, pussy, screw,* and a few others are emotionally loaded. A few years ago just one of those words carried around on a poster at the University of California almost turned that venerable institu-tion into a Roman ruin. By the time the riots, protests, investiga-tions, and outraged-taxpayer letters to the editor had run their course, everyone had become a believer in the power of the printed word—four-letter variety. I have my own explanation for the hysterical reaction as well as the discomfort of so many to these words: They cut down the emotional distance between people. I can say, "I enjoy marital relations with my husband" to the ladies of the Thursday morning poetry and paint-by-numbers ladies group without increasing their adrenalin flow one bit. But if I get closer to them and to my subject and tell them, "I love fucking my man and being fucked by him," they'll have to summon the respirator crew. It would get too close to where it's at. They won't be able to remain detached from their own fearful feelings. When we were told there were nice words and there were dirty words, of course, nobody said *why* they were dirty. They didn't know. But they were dead set against them and against those awful people who used them. And we grew up feeling very naughty whenever we whispered one. Does that have anything to do with why we find the words arousing? We all know it does. But if the no-no attitudes are still strongly with us, we won't be able to find any kicks in them. Then we'll be stuck with that dry old clinical language or no talk at all.

This can create a problem or two for our sex. We're supposed to be ladies (well, aren't we?), and ladies don't use such words. Ladies are not even supposed to know what they mean. The high school boys didn't know girls wrote the same words on the walls of the girl's room that boys scrawled on the walls of the boy's room. And we kept them in boy-girl-game ignorance. Would you believe it? I've talked with gals five years or more married who still had their husbands believing they didn't know the meaning of that four-letter word we learned when we were about eight. One guy told me he had to tell his wife what it meant when their teen-age son used it! Now what sort of cloistered-little-virgin role do you suppose she was trying to play? The trouble is, such women had sold men such a bill of goods their guys would be shocked into a coma to hear them say, "I love feeling your prick in my cunt." So, where does this leave us when it comes to talking about sex and exchanging thoughts on what we like or dislike in love-making? Absolutely nowhere, unless we can find some way to break through the communication wall. Of course, one can always try to rely on sensual braille, which is fun, but it sometimes leads to misinterpretations. If you have the problem, try writing him a letter telling him of all the great things he does to you. Make it explicit, *very* explicit, but whatever you do, don't air your gripes; if you do, you will build the wall even higher. Let him know those words which turn you on. Use them in your letter. In other words, turn on your feminine creativity and compose a lengthy erotic tome. Don't worry about literary talent. You can almost certainly outwrite the porno novelists. (Come to think of it, you might discover a source of added money as a writer: "Be the first on your block to write dirty books!") You can then wind up your love letter by telling him how much you would enjoy having him talk to you of sex. And how much it would turn you on.

When it comes to talking *during* sex, I think it can be a definite turn-on, an annoying distraction, or a decided turn-off. I can't imagine keeping my passions at peak level if he decides to talk office politics while making love to me. And if I wait until I climb between the sheets with him to tell him all the exciting trivia of my day, I may find myself with a man who goes for sleep rather than sex. I also don't think that during sex is the appropriate time for tender words of affection. Some of those syrupy old marriage manuals advise husbands to speak beautiful words of love during the act, "reassuring your wife of your deepest feelings of love." Personally, if my man went into a "how do I love thee? let me count the ways" routine while giving me a good ride on the water bed, I would be sure he had lost his mind or his interest in sex. At that point, I'm interested solely in fucking and being fucked, in that stiff, hard organ of his making me feel good, and in letting myself go in response to him. It's a glorious primitive feeling, not the sentiment of a lace valentine. Any whispering of "I love you, my dearest. Do you love me?" would distract both of us. And who needs distractions at a time like that? Verbalizing your reactions to the good things he is doing to you, however, can enhance his pleasure. A woman's passionate demand, "Fuck me! Fuck me! Fuck me!" is a real turn-on to most men during love-making. And I think the majority of men enjoy hearing that murmured "God! Your cock feels good!" no matter how many times they've heard it before. Furthermore, the girl who lets her man know her feelings in those explicit terms isn't likely to be asked, "Did it happen for you?" afterward.

Of course, some couples do talk about sex, but maybe they shouldn't. All they ever talk about is what's wrong with it, what they aren't getting out of it, and what they think they deserve to get. All of which is as joyless as an income tax audit. If something is less than right in your love life, sure you want to improve it, and talking is the first step. But bitching isn't. Unless a gal is just totally turned-off by everything sexual, or can't stomach the man she's with, she'll find a lot of things he does trigger a lot of positive responses. If she makes a point of talking about those goodies and how very good they make her feel, she is almost sure to accomplish two goals: First, it will encourage him to give her even more of what she likes; and second, she can then tactfully let him know if something turns her off. (I'm not suggesting, however, that you go through any "It didn't happen to me" routine if that is a common occurrence and you know of no specific actions he can take to change it. Frigidity, or what

Masters and Johnson call *orgasmic dysfunction,* isn't something which can be cured by suggesting he try a few different techniques. It's the woman's problem as much, or more, than the man's and professional help is usually the answer.)

You might also try some sharing games for sexual communication. In their book, *Total Sex* (Peter H. Wyden, Inc., New York, 1972), Herbert and Roberta Otto suggest the couple share their far-out fantasies. "*Invariably sexual fantasies,*" they say, "*present an important creative communication possibility.* The sharing of sexual fantasies can bring greater openness to communication and often has a marked effect on the sex life of partners. The basic ground rule of all sex-fantasy communication involves an agreement by both partners that *all* sexual fantasies that occur when the couple is together will be shared verbally. Also included are important sexual fantasies that occur when the couple is not together. This is done with the clear understanding that *sharing a sexual fantasy does not necessarily have any implication for action.*" (Italics are the authors'.) I agree such sharing might provide an added something to sex, but I emphasize the word *might.* I think I might get just a little bit uptight if my man kept telling me his fantasies of that big-boobed gal in the typing pool!

One of the women in the Ottos' sample described the man in her fantasy as "very strong, firm, and very gentle. He delights in forcing enjoyment on me. Although I'm begging him to stop he knows I don't want him to. The more I beg, the more determined he becomes. *His penis is very large and it fills my entire body.* I cannot escape him. . . ." (Italics *mine!*) With the uncertainty so many men have over the size of that male organ of theirs, that fantasy could be devastating.

We can say fantasies do not necessarily have any implications for action, but can we say they have no implications for desired action? Of course not, since that is really what fantasies are all about. If you share fantasies which tell your partner you would prefer sharing your bed with someone else, the relationship certainly is not going to be enhanced. Look at it this way: Suppose

you have a 32A bust, and your man repeatedly shares fantasies
of playing mattress games with a gal who measures a magnifi-
cent 38D. You can tell yourself he loves you, and only you, and
that you offer him many more assets than a pair of expanded
mammaries. But those fantasies don't add to your feelings of being desirable, do they? I'd say if there is any danger your
fantasies might give him the idea he is not the man of your
erotic dreams, keep them to yourself. And if he really isn't what
you want in a man, what's keeping you? I have an alternative
suggestion. Share fantasies and special memories of what each
of you would like to do for the other one and have the other
one do for you. Or to you. Or with you. I have a favorite variation on it. I like to make bets. On almost anything and everything: football games, poker hands, race horses, and the year the
Bastille fell. I bet with that man of mine, and the bet is always
the same. The one who wins gets to plan and carry out making
love to the other any way he or she desires. When I win (which
is usual—I cheat a lot), I plan all sorts of erotic games with
which to pleasure him. A part of the fun, then, is relaxing before
the fireplace with a glass of wine—before we start anything—and
telling him, in detail, all the things I plan to do. And when he
wins, he does the same. It builds expectations, increases fantasies, and is just generally a great turn-on. Where the shared
fantasies come in is when we create erotic plans which will
probably never be carried out but which might turn the other
one on. Let's say you think your man might be turned-on by
fantasies of an evening with a couple of girls in a Japanese bath
house. You could describe in detail all the things they would do
for him and how they would do it. The great part of fantasies is
that they don't have to be limited to what may be practical or
safe. So long as neither of you is likely to be hurt by envy,
insecurity, or whatever, and you won't be if you keep in mind
fantasies are only fantasies; you can build the daydreams into a
De Mille production in living color. The fact that you give him a
fantasy tale of those oriental bathing gals doesn't mean you are
urging him to buy an airline ticket to Tokyo. Even sex fantasies

which some of us might think of as "kinky sex" are still only fantasies. Maybe you know he gets turned-on by fantasies of "bondage" sex, that business of making out with a gal after first tying her up in a chair or spread-eagle on the bed, and the whole idea leaves you turned-off but good. Should you start looking in the phone directory for a sanitarium in which to have your lover incarcerated? Or pack your bag and set a date with a lawyer? Not unless you want to toss in the towel on all men. They all have fantasies. (So do we—admit it!) If he wants to tie you down while he drives you out of your senses with erotic pleasuring, why object. It might not be your thing, but you won't suffer from it. And if it remains strictly a fantasy, well, you won't even experience it. Even if he has fantasies of whips, leather, and the whole sadomasochistic scene, so long as they stay just fantasies, why get upset? You can make up spanking tales for him and turn him on, yet still draw the line where it gets too far-out and kinky for you. Fantasies are one thing; actions are another.

As for humor in sex, I think the oh-so-serious approach to loving is just about the worst thing that can happen to a man and woman. It would take Freud himself to explain it. It probably has something to do with embarrassment, or inhibitions, or, God help us all, a lack of any sense of humor. Why humor? Well, beyond what I mentioned about humor being tied in with joy and joy being a sexual thing—or is it the other way around—and the fact that a damn good roll in the hay makes me smile all the following day, there is another good reason humor should never be left out: It makes sex so very *human.* Ever think about the fact that humans are the only animals who smile or laugh. Furthermore, just about everything we do in sex is really funny if we stop to think of it. All those weird positions and bizarre actions are pretty hilarious. And we all have had experiences in sex which, if we are honest about it, are laughable. So why not enjoy a good laugh? I'm sure I don't need to point out, however, that the idea is to laugh *with* him, never *at* him. If you find his amorous overtures hilariously funny and you let him know it, you know what the outcome will be; and who wants to sleep alone?

Ever since the word "games" became a part of cocktail party psychoanalysis, everybody seems to be uptight about fun and games of any sort. And sex leads the parade. Males and females used to be able to accept the obvious: that sex is a whole lot of fun; it feels good; and it is by far the greatest game a couple can play. Ten times better than bridge. A game at which everyone wins. But now, I'm beginning to fear we may kill it with *seriousness*. On the one side, we have those who insist on making the whole business a collection of problems. Women's magazines are beginning to read like reruns of Masters and Johnson. And instead of playing games in the back seat of a car, college kids are rapping about "meaningful relationships" and their place in the astrological cosmos. Everybody waded through the tedious masturbation adventures of pathetic Portnoy. And except for the Jewish mamas, the readers loved it into best-sellerdom. Even porno movies have gotten into the deadly serious trap. When they aren't examining the psychology of something or other "relevant" or killing off threescore fallen damsels, they are mechanically oscillating with perpetually dour expressions. They look as if they're living up to the agreement of a suicide pact. I say let's bring fun and games back to sex before we kill it off.

I won't try to suggest a list of games a couple might play. A book on *Games People Play—With Their Clothes Off* might be a welcome addition to the bedroom library, but this isn't the book. Besides, I think the games we come up with ourselves, often spontaneously, are the most fun. I recently heard of a party game on the market which might become the Monopoly for grown-up boys and girls. You spin a dial or draw a card or some such thing and all those various sex acts are described and/or pictured. Whichever one loses (?!) has to come through with the action called for. A little like strip poker—carried all the way. I think the idea sounds like fun, but I don't see why a couple couldn't devise such a game for themselves and save the money. I've heard of (and tried) a number of very creative games couples have come up with. One pair came up with this one: With a marking pencil, they each would write a sex act or position on their own lower abdomen, not letting the other one know what they had written. They then put their clothes on and play a game of strip poker. When finally the bikini pants come off, the loser wins: The winner follows the instructions off the partner's anatomy. I suppose if the preferences are too involved and complex, they can always number them and then just write a number. For the athletes, there is always tag, leap frog, wrestling, and go-go dancing. And speaking of dancing, a few years ago a school for belly dancing opened in San Francisco and quickly discovered most of their enrollees were not would-be professionals: They were housewives who saw the art as offering additional fun in the bedroom. A school for strippers in Los Angeles found the same thing and finally pitched all their advertising to the suburban wife who might improve her skill in disrobing. And for those who might not be able to take advantage of such advanced education, one company produced a long-playing record with instruction book for learning how to strip to music "in the privacy of your own home." Great idea, I'd say. Just about every man enjoys the turn-on of a strip-tease if it projects a healthy quantity of eroticism. When it is *his* woman giving him a private show, well, we know what it can do, don't we? For those of us who feel somewhat insecure in our stripping skills, maybe such a school or instruction book is the answer. Simply imitating professionals we have seen may help. And in the afternoons, one can practice nude dancing alone in front of a full-length mirror. For us narcissists (and aren't we all?), this can be a turn-on in itself.

Sharing laughs over sex, like sharing fantasies, is best done in the nude. Not always, of course. Variety is still the magic word. But sitting on the floor facing each other before the fire, with a bowl of fruit between you, with nothing on but a little perfume and firelight, sharing delightfully erotic thoughts, is, well, you think of an appropriate word.

Come to think of it, just about everything a man and woman can do in privacy with clothes on can be done in the nude—

except maybe frying fish. A formal dinner for two *au naturel,* with candlelight, wine, and your most elaborate dinner service, is a great way to celebrate a special occasion like ground hog day or Martin Van Buren's birthday. And then, of course, a man is built just right when he is aroused for a gal to play a game of ring toss, even though she doesn't have the proper equipment to give him a turn. Johnny Carson did a take off on some suggestions of mine in a previous book, a work written for men who want to pleasure women. They absolutely broke me up. "Cover her with guacomole; remove it with a taco chip." "Massage her behind the knees with an egg beater." Following the broadcast, someone asked me if I wasn't annoyed at Johnny for turning the serious business of sexual love into a subject for humor. My answer: Never! I think humor should *always* be kept in sex. I have never understood people who can find laughs in mother-in-law jokes (when in-laws are no laughing matter for many couples) but get uptight and "offended" by sexual jokes. One of the funniest movies I've ever seen was a nudie Western. And I think the only sad thing about the vast majority of porno movies is their total lack of humor. Woody Allen has given us a glimpse of what such a movie could be, but Woody has stayed within the limits. Oh well, things are changing. Maybe before long we will find acceptance for some genuinely funny sex films.

Speaking of sex films, erotic-movie viewing is another delightful thing a couple can do in the nude. Not in your neighborhood X-rated theater, of course; not even San Francisco is that liberal. Porno films can be purchased and/or rented in most major cities for viewing with your home projector, and in the past few years the quality has improved greatly over those grainy old flicks the boys used to watch on stag night. The two of you can start your own collection and have something to choose from besides TV reruns.

And one more fun suggestion: Plan a literary evening. Have him stretch out while you read to him from a collection of erotic writings. I'll grant it is hard to find well-written porno writing, especially writing with a touch of humor. I think some of the best is found in the Victorian erotic tales. It can be found, however, if you search around, and it doesn't have to be the sickie stuff. You can sprawl out side-by-side reading your favorite stories, but I'll bet he finds his biggest kick in having you read to him from a collection of strong, turn-on bedtime stories.

12
His Other World—and Yours

To all the other nonsense we learned about sex, we can add *The Myth of the Perpetual Erection.* It's kept in vogue by our unfortunate sisters who just can't stand sex. We've all heard them: "George is interested in nothing but sex. Why, if he had his way, we would do nothing but you-know-what all day long!" She should be so lucky! But we all know better. Show me the man who is interested in nothing but sex, and I'll show you a mental dwarf with overactive glands. Show me the gal who claims her man can perform for breakfast, lunch, dinner, and a late-night snack, and I'll show you a prevaricating little bragger.

As a matter of genuine fact, the opposite would be no myth at all. For every woman complaining that her man won't let her alone, I'll bet there are 17.5 gals biting their nails to the forearms because they are left alone far too much. Most men have a way of filling their lives up to the brim with very-very-very-important ambitious pursuits. When they aren't engaged in simultaneously climbing three different Mount Everests, they are busily studying the plans for assaulting a fourth mountain. All of which leaves us trying to catch them on the run and seduce them into a time-out for loving. I know there are some guys with ambition to do nothing more than test mattresses—but I don't know any, and to the gal who has one for a mate, all I can say is, "I hope you go for the quiet life; I don't."

I'll assume your man is a lot like mine. He has another world in which he spends what for me is a frustrating amount of time. I can share a part of it—sometimes—but for the most part, it's his world. It is filled with job, investments, plans, and projects. I may manipulate him into an afternoon on a beach with me, but I can't be sure his mind won't keep jumping to something from the *Wall Street Journal* or a plan for a vacation hut in the Leeward Islands. He's like most men, and most men live in the future. Sure, it can be frustrating, but his work to bring those plans through gives me both security and the satisfactions of living with a man.

I will be the first to admit, however, that his busy world can be a pain in the neck. When he brings a dictating machine along on an Acapulco vacation, or talks of tax shelters while sharing cocktails in the sunset, I can come close to losing my cool. I've tried several ploys designed to bring him back to me, to say, "Hey! Remember me? I've missed you. Won't you turn off that busy world of yours and just join me in feeling close and all warm inside?" Most of my schemes haven't worked; a few only make matters worse. I might try nagging. It's supposed to be the *modus operandi* of our sex. But I don't. We all know men welcome that less than a case of boils. Furthermore, even if it works, it doesn't work. It turns into "Win the battle and lose the war." About the third time you say, "You never pay any attention to me," he might put down his copy of *Sports Illustrated* with a sigh: "O.K., what is it you want?" But where do you go from there? You can be sure it *won't* be into his amorous arms! Or you can be coy and cute and try to distract him from his thoughts of how to snag the "big contract" from his competitor. You know, slip into that near-transparent baby doll and plop your perfumed little bottom on his lap, push your tongue in his ear, and make sounds like a kitten in heat. You just might get him to put down the newspaper—if you're not sitting on it—but how many times can you use that little-girl-sexpot ploy? About the third time running, you may find your little bottom bounced on the floor. A man likes being seduced, but he doesn't like being *had*—in the name of seduction. If you are a believer in the straight-on approach, you can always come right out and make it a demand: "Hey, lover, pay attention to me—or else!" There is a good chance it may work—sometimes. Two possible drawbacks here: Unless you have a line on a new man, you can only cry wolf with that "or else" business just so many times, and what do you answer when he comes back with, "O.K., I'm all ears. Now what do you want to talk about?" And let us not expect to peak the male interest with dumb-dumb chitchat and domestic drivel.

So that's where the other alternative comes in. Don't fight him; join him. That's right. Become a part of his world. Or at least know his world well enough to be able to talk with him—*and have him want to talk with you.*

First, we have to *know* the world of our men. And that means knowing their interests, schemes, dreams, and worries. I don't care what anyone says, being a good conversationalist means more than just being a patient listener. Unless your man is on some kind of incredible ego trip, he won't be satisfied giving a monologue, listening to the sound of his own voice, and playing teacher to his little-girl pupil all the time. If a gal cannot offer a fair exchange in conversation, she can expect to lose out to the TV set or the bowling league, everywhere but in bed—and maybe even there. But let me see if I can anticipate most of the feminine objections when this is suggested (because I'm far from the first to come up with it): "My man is an astrophysical engineer working on a top-secret project for breeding long-haired llamas on Mars, and I can't understand anything about his job." "Every fall, I'm a football widow. He's a nut on football but I'm just not interested in it. It just looks like a bunch of men running around knocking one another down." "He's always coming up with some wild scheme for making a million, or coming home with talk about us sailing a boat to Tahiti. I get so tired of him being up in the clouds, I just turn him off." "I'd be happy if my man would talk about *anything;* he's the original Silent Sam: I have to drag every word out of him."

Shall we take a look at the gripes from the top? Does she really have to take a degree in astrophysical engineering in order to talk with her man? Not unless he's a walking slide rule with nothing between his scalp but blueprints and figures (and not the female variety). Assuming she isn't intellectually impoverished, she should be able to grasp at least the essentials of his work. The schools today are even teaching the fundamentals of Einstein's theory of relativity to grammar school kids. Besides, he almost surely has other things in his world they can share. If all he can talk about is his work, why did she get tied up with him in the first place? I'll give you odds he talks more than shop when he brown-bags with the other engineers at lunch.

As for that football-widow business, isn't it a big fat bore? Aren't all clichés? It's just one more example of that dumb sex stereotyping that taught us there was something called "woman talk," and little girls play with dolls while little boys climb trees, and guys dig football while their women prefer ballet. If she doesn't know any more about football than "a bunch of men running around knocking one another down," why doesn't she improve her education? Sure, we know the answer, don't we? "But I don't like football." And that's an answer? Not if she wants him. If he wants football and she wants him, she'll be cuddled up against him watching the quarterback set up for a screen pass and talking about whether the zone defense has taken some of the excitement out of the game. That's what red chips are all about.

The next one really pushes up my blood pressure. I've never been able to make sense of it, but so many women seem to get their perverse kicks out of stepping on dreams—if the dreams belong to their men. So he comes home with dreams of sailing to Tahiti. There's a crime in that? Take away our dreams and what do we have left? Yet here is some bitchy broad just waiting to pour ice water on her man any time he dares to dream. Where do you find more poison than that? I've heard the excuses these gals offer. "But all I try to do is bring him back to reality." "But if I didn't say something, he'd have me off in a dinghy in the middle of the ocean—and he doesn't know a thing about sailing." What a lot of bleep that is. Coming home with beautiful dreams of Tahiti is a long, long way from taking her aboard a boat, and unless she believes he is a congenital idiot, she doesn't fear he is going to sail off with her into the sunset the next day. Dreams can become plans, which can become goals. But most of our dreams remain just that, dreams. When he finally asks her to cast off the bowline, she can then decide whether she wants to stay a landlubber. The gal with forty-two cents worth of brains joins her man in his dreams; she doesn't jump on them.

And how does our fatuous filly react to her man's schemes to make a million? She starts talking about security. "He's always coming up with these wild ideas that would risk everything we have. Don't I have the right to protect myself (and the children)?" Ask her how many times she has had to go hungry or sleep on the sidewalk since she has been with him. But even if he has gone belly up on a venture or two in the past, would she rather have a man with what J. Paul Getty has called a "civil-service mentality"? Show me a man who won't take risks to achieve his goals, and I'll show you a guy who will score no points with his gal—or with any others. Maybe he'll never invent the hula hoop or hit for a bundle on the stock market, but give me a guy who thinks big. I'll gamble with him. And on him. And if we go broke? Well, what the hell, loving in the out-of-doors and roasting hot dogs over a beach fire can be more fun than preparing a banquet spread.

What about the gal who finds herself with a guy who seldom says more than "What's in the mail?" She has a lot of company, although I doubt it consoles her much. They may not all be strong, silent types, but there are an awful lot of silent males around. And an equal number of frustrated females clawing the furniture because "He never talks to me." Is there anything a gal can do about it? Maybe yes; maybe no. Some guys just don't like talking, in the same way some don't like dancing or playing table tennis. But if that is the man she is talking about, what complaint has she? Didn't she know what he was like after the first evening? And if so, didn't she want what she got? My bet would be that she got *part* of the package she was after and was willing to settle for that—at first. He may have been good in bed, or heavy of bankroll, and she was willing to take him, silence and all. Now she's unhappy with the deal she made, but not unhappy enough to give up those fringe benefits he offers. My advice to her is to make her choice: Take him the way he is, or roll up her negligee in her sleeping bag and hit the road. But don't try to nag him into being a different man. It won't work. That case isn't typical, however. In the more common situation, he did talk when they first got together. The conversation flowed like New Year's Eve champagne. But then gradually the flow slowed down and came close to drying up altogether. What happened? Was it the obvious? They just ran out of things to talk about? Could be. One can't make an omelette without eggs. And without informational input, how long can two people go on talking without insufferable boredom? I don't like to generalize, but I'm afraid our sex often scores a big zero when it comes to making a conversational contribution to our men. Maybe most men don't have much more to talk about, but they seem to—at least the men I'm around. I've often wondered, for example, who ever started this idiocy called "girl talk" in which mindless broads can sit around over their coffee cups and talk about nothing but chintz curtains, changing hem lengths, cake mixes, and children, or how women came to turn on soap operas and turn off all interests above the level of a slow-witted ten-year-old. Housewives who never read anything in the newspaper except Dear Abby, the horoscope, and the women's page. Secretaries who sit mindlessly turning the pages of confession magazines during their lunch hour. Unbelievable! O.K., so maybe there are just as many men who choose to live with mental malnutrition, but this book isn't written to men; we're talking only about what we gals do and don't do. Besides, even if she is married to a certified clod, does she have to join him in dumbsville? If I haven't learned anything, had any ideas, read anything of interest to him, and have just generally shut down my brain for the day, I can't expect him to have much to say beyond "When do we eat?" when he walks through the door. If he's a golf freak and I don't know a nine iron from a vaulting pole, you can bet I'm going to change things. And I sure don't mean I'm going to nag him off the golf course or give an opening to some female who can talk with him on how to break par for three hours at a cocktail party. Not on your love life. I'm going to get off my mental tail and turn *myself* into the gal he can share three hours of golf talk with. I'm no fool. I know what it will buy me: HIM! What's more, I will have found one more interest to add to *my* life. We also are not going to talk long if he brings up something about world politics and all I know about it is what I can remember from a high school class in history. Or if, when he says something about the stock market, I answer with a grunt and then change the subject to a leaky kitchen faucet.

There is an even better explanation of why some guys have so little to say to their women: They have learned better. Let a man get put down, ridiculed, or cut up when he expresses an opinion, and it won't take him long to learn it is safer to keep quiet. We have all seen those couples who hang in there with one of those "It's raining"—"Don't be stupid! The sun is shining" relationships. No matter what the guy says, he is likely to find it shot down by Little Miss Know-it-all. When she isn't trying to impress him with her encyclopedic knowledge of damn near everything, she is castrating him with her corrections. She spends time puzzling over how such a beautiful genius could have tied up with such a male moron. She can't understand why he seems disinterested in talking with her when she so obviously has so much to offer him.

Or what about the guy who gets hit with hostility every time he opens his mouth? I can't think of a reason for him to keep trying. Can you? If out of a hundred topics which could once be discussed, eighty or ninety have become too touchy, conversation may be as welcome as cockroaches in the bedroom. The psychologists call it defensiveness, and I'll go along with their name for it, but you'll pardon me if I just call such a gal a nasty little bitch. She has this hangup on trying to prove she can always score one-up on a man, especially the poor jerk she shares her bed with—when she hasn't thrown him out on his fanny. Maybe it is, like they say, her attempt to compensate for some feelings of inferiority, but it seems to me that if it is, acting like a scaly witch isn't the way to get to be any less inferior. And it sure isn't any way to get a man to want to talk, let alone love. It seems to me some couples do to conversational topics what they do to vacation spots: They manage to screw up just about every one. They could go on a world tour and manage to come back with a soured taste for every spot they visited. They can return with memories of fighting in thirty-seven cities in five languages including profane. Keep it up for a few years and they can run out of world.

Every expert mistress and courtesan has learned one thing and learned it well: how to talk to a man. She knows she isn't going to keep a guy interested with just what she has between her legs. And regardless of what Mom told her, her ability with rare steak also isn't enough. But if she has the rest of it all together and she can talk with him about what turns him on and make him know she is interested in what interests him, he'll buy her the Taj Mahal. Ever see a photo of Mata Hari? A Raquel Welch she was not, but she had what it takes to charm the secrets out of some high military brass. And they say Cleopatra was a dog and that they really had to rewrite history when they cast Liz Taylor Burton in the part, but she sure had that something which keeps a man interested. And you can bet a big part of it was an ability to stay tuned in and turned on by what he had to say. And to have something to say in return that wasn't boring or bitchy. It's a cinch Cleo never prattled on about the new drapes she planned for her barge on the Nile.

So it's stupid to fight his world and it can be fun to join it, but what about our world? Haven't most of us felt, at one time or other, that our men don't give a rancid fig for our interests?

When they talk for three hours of disc brakes and carburetors, we are expected to stay wide-eyed and panting, right? And when they fill an evening with details of the office politics, we are supposed to find it as exciting as sky diving, right? And if the guy comes to bed with a scheme for beating the income taxes by investing in an Alaskan magnesium mine, his woman is expected to rub his back while he plots his war with the IRS, right? It's that old subservient-role-of-woman bit, right? Fair is fair, isn't it? Why shouldn't we expect—even demand—that *they* show as much interest in our world? Well, I won't argue the ultimate justice of the argument, but, frankly, I like to live in reality and my reality tells me *he* isn't going to be excited by what goes to make up my world if all that goes to make up my world is the bleep which fills the pages of women's magazines (at least most women's magazines). And I can't fault him for *that*. But if I want to seriously interest him in something which has more intellectual content than a PTA meeting, I better give some thought to salesmanship—content, presentation, and packaging. Americans go on vacation in Mexico or Spain and watch their first bullfight. They return to Omaha and New Rochelle and tell their friends how barbaric the whole business is. And judging from the bullfight they probably witnessed, I can't disagree. I've seen bulls slaughtered in the Plaza de Toros in Madrid in ways which couldn't be gorier, and by supposedly top-ranked matadors. But if one swallow doesn't make a summer, one bad bullfight doesn't make the corrida a sadistic blood bath. If the tourist is fortunate enough to witness a truly great bullfight, chances are he will be hooked on the ancient art and become a true *aficionado*. Now let's say I'm a nut on symphonic music and my man is strictly a jazz buff. I may talk him into taking me to a concert of Beethoven, Mozart, and Bach, but I seriously doubt he will walk out eager to buy season tickets. Like oysters and oral sex, it's an acquired taste. But a pops concert of music from motion picture themes and Broadway musicals might go down pretty easy and smooth the way for an introduction to heavier music. And whether we like it or not, we may have to face up to that brainwashed masculine image. The guy who has been raised to see manhood in the mold of Ernest Hemingway, John Wayne, and Genghis Khan would rather be caught sneaking into a bordello than a ballet performance. But telling him he has a masculinity hangup isn't going to help the gal's cause. If she has a passionate thing for the ballet, *and* she plays her red chips stacked high and over the long haul, he may eventually break down and discover that an evening at the ballet isn't going to turn him into a fairy. And if he never does submit to two hours of *Swan Lake?* Well, she can go off to the theater by herself, or she can find something to do with him that will beat anything ever put on the stage.

Personally, I dig having a man who takes a genuine interest in my world. But not every crummy little half acre of it. I like cooking, and I have enough cookbooks to stock a library in a school of culinary arts. He has more than the usual male interest in eating, gourmet and otherwise (although a thick steak, medium rare, is more apt to turn him on than some dish with three French names that takes four hours in a deep tureen). But I certainly don't expect him to sit with me browsing through the pages of Julia Child's latest work on cookery. And he doesn't expect me to be up on the latest thing in tax shelters and stock splits. But when it comes to things like women's clothes, well, yes, I want him to share my world. And he does. I know all the tired clichés about men hating to go shopping with a woman, and I am convinced they carry some truth. Most men I know decide what they want, walk in the store and buy it, and the whole transaction, including "shopping," is completed in less time than it takes most of our sex to find a salesclerk. And that seems especially true when it comes to shopping for clothes, probably because until recently men haven't been offered much variety in the clothes they wear. They can't understand how a woman can spend an entire day trying on twenty-seven dresses and not find a thing. And if they get dragged along on such an expedition into frustration, they come out of it numb with exhaustion. If you have a man who actually enjoys this

sort of thing, you have reason to feel uneasy; he may be strange
in other ways as well. When I dress, I want to dress for my man,
in clothes which will turn him on. And that goes for anything
and everything I wear, even something I put on to paint the
bathroom. So naturally I keep my eyes open to what makes his
eyes open. With that as my measure, I can eliminate 90 per cent
of the things available in any store. Then out of the 10 per cent
or less which might fill the requirements, I can select the ones I
want to show him. I can usually take them home on approval
and give him a private showing. If not, I may persuade him into
going to the store with me if I have those three or four dresses
picked out and waiting. It hasn't failed yet.

Of course, I have a lot more to my world than just clothes and
such. And so do you. You may have a career which occupies at
least half your waking hours, one that is more than just a job.
How do you share that part of your world? Or should a gal even
try? I guess my answer would have to be: That depends on
several things. For one thing, shoptalk, if carried to an extreme,
is a fat bore, regardless of the "shop" being talked about. Even
if you are in a "glamour" job, can you be sure he wants to listen
to daily details of your exciting job (if there is such a thing)?
Personally, I've yawned my way through evenings of shoptalk
with some less than exciting personalities from motion pictures,
advertising, television, publishing, the arts, and a few other pro-
fessions and occupations supposedly touched with glamour. I
long ago decided there is no such thing as a glamorous, exciting
job. There are only people who think some jobs are more exciting and glamorous than the job they hold. But even if you do
hold a one-in-a-million job filled with fascinating people and
events, you may want to consider how much time you spend
telling him all the details. If we are interested in men, we can
never afford to forget that complex male ego. Whether we want
to call it a chauvinistic hangup or whatever, men have a definite
thing about being king of the hill, and if our men get the idea
we are trying to take over the mountain peak, we may find ourselves filing applications in the spinsters' home. Let a man feel

his woman is trying to top him, and he may go off in search of a smarter woman.

If a woman is supposed to be interested in her man's work and his climb up the corporate ladder, shouldn't he show an equal interest in her career? It's only fair, right? I agree. But if there is one thing I've learned about boy-girl games, it is that fairness doesn't buy much. And trying to talk with most men about what may or may not be fair is a fine way *not* to score feminine points. Personally, so long as he gives me what I want as a woman, I won't worry about equality, justice, or anything else. Every man wants to believe he is absolutely the center of his woman's life. Not just the most important thing; the *only* thing. He will probably take pride in her accomplishments and brag about them to the other guys, but between the two of them, he wants to know he is number one. I think a gal could be president of General Motors without anything being taken away from what she has with her man, but only if she could succeed in convincing him he was more important to her than her position in the executive suite. The woman who could pull that off could rule the world.

Most of us have our hands full trying to manage even one small outside activity while keeping our man satisfied. A gal will take the job of Den Mother to the Cub Scouts, and she will become more active than Henry Kissinger. Her man will have to put up with an entire dinner conversation of Cub Pack activities. And he will have to face a TV dinner while he listens. Den Mother couldn't break away from the pack in time to prepare anything else. And you know, I actually think such broads expect their men to bounce up and down with enthusiasm for their involvements. I don't care who the man is, if he is normal, and he cares at all for his woman and isn't simply trying to get her to become involved in something so he will be free to pursue something on his own, he can, and will, react with jealousy whenever he feels she puts something or someone ahead of him. Period. That could mean children, job, hobby, community involvement, or just about anything else.

My advice on conversation: If the topic is an interest which is yours alone—*your* job, *your* hobby, *your* relatives, *your* organization—COOL IT! You don't have to try to keep the whole thing a deep, dark secret. If you do, he may start thinking you have something going at work that you want to keep hidden behind the file cabinets. Just don't fill the air with *your* happenings and interests in which he doesn't share. It's as much a matter of enthusiasm as anything else. Of all the stupid moves a woman can make, just about the dumbest (provided she wants to keep her man) is to show enthusiasm when she talks about her activities, but act bored when she is with him. He can talk about taking her on a Caribbean cruise and she'll sit there in a glassy-eyed stupor, her response a little less lively than a comatose tortoise. But she can light up like an opening night when she gushes about what the boss said or gives a monologue of details on the happenings of her Women's Society for the Preservation of Endangered Aardvarks.

Men have been told they are male chauvinist pigs enough times in recent years, many of them are beginning to believe it. They are developing guilt feelings over being male and even joining feminist organizations so they can attend meetings where they can be hung from the rafters by their balls while they beat their breasts in guilt over being possessed of a penis. It's part of the chronic guilt neurosis of the insecure intellectual. So of course he learns to say all the acceptable, liberal lines: "I don't expect to be everything in her life. She has a lot of drive and many interests besides our relationship. I can't ask her to be thinking of me all the time. I try to encourage and support her in her activities." But anyone who believes him is in as much trouble as he is. Give him enough time in that brainwashed, liberal-guilt state and he'll begin spending time in businessmen's bars wondering how good a lay the cocktail waitress might be. That's not for me. I'll take a man who has his head on straight enough to be able to admit he wants to possess his woman and keep her eyes turned on him before all else. A male chauvinist? Probably. But a tiger when and where it's important. And I'll ride on that. But good.

13
Strictly for Green-eyed Girls

If that picture we are given of ancient Rome isn't overdrawn, orgies sure aren't what they used to be. You know, all those gladiators in short togas stretched out on pillows with a collection of gals, all with great bodies, feeding them grapes and lust. I doubt if all the defense lobbyists in Washington rolled together could put together a bash like that these days. Even if they could, who would they invite? A few Pentagon generals with flab rolls and sweaty palms, a senile senator or two, a few bellicose congressmen, a woman's-lib-type newspaper columnist, a fag television producer, and assorted gate-crashing drunks? Think it would make a "Playboy Goes to a Party" pictorial? Not even a feature in the underground press. No matter how far underground.

Anyway, today nobody gives orgies. I mean, when was the last time you were invited to a lavish night of reveling in the altogether? No, neither have I. Now there are swingers, would-be swingers, and patrons of movies about swingers. If you believe some of what you hear and read, you might get the idea everybody these days is playing musical beds. Adultery games have replaced bridge. And neighbors borrow mates like they used to borrow garden tools.

Well I, for one, don't believe it. I'm sure adultery has been with the human race longer than the common cold. The early

Greeks did more than their share of playing around. So did the Egyptians. And the Old Testament is filled with tales of straying husbands and wives. What's so new when somebody tacks the name "swinging" on it? Actually not much. Except the "swingers" try to turn adultery into an institution—and try to sell it to the rest of us who are already bored with institutions. They run around interviewing one another, telling the uninitiated how swinging relieves boredom, saves flagging marriages, and contributes to world peace. Then the art director of a girlie magazine illustrates the article with photos of models who look nothing at all like the participants in a swinging party. Come to think of it, they look just like girlie magazine models.

And what do the real swingers look like? Well, whatever a winner looks like, that isn't it. Pink-cheeked, flabby little businessmen, middle-aged housewives trying desperately to hang on to a high school cheerleader image, bisexuals who can't seem to score well with either sex. But genuine lovers? Forget it! Pathetic males who are impotent with their wives join swingers group where they are impotent with other men's wives. Frigid clubwomen climb in the sack with some stray male at the party and find—surprise!—they still can't reach orgasm.

A noted sexologist, who shall remain nameless out of pity, wrote a piece a couple of years ago presenting what he called a "rational argument for intelligent adultery." Only two things wrong with it: It was not rational, and certainly not very intelligent. I think an argument against marriage might be sensible. God knows, if marriage means what most couples I see have going for them (or against them), I can't think of one rational reason for getting into it. The tedious grin-and-bear-it routine of connubial "bliss" they opt for is right out of a combination situation comedy and horror film. I think anyone willing to settle for *that* is in need of a keeper. But just because such a marriage is irrational, adultery doesn't become more rational. If I'm not getting what I want from my man and I figure I probably won't get what I want in the future, I'm not going to hang around to be chewed up by frustration and hostility. And if I can't, or won't, provide what he wants from a woman, I would expect him to have enough sense to clear out.

Nevertheless, irrational or not, a lot of playing around does go on, and we might as well face up to it and understand how and why this is so. I don't want to share *my* man with *anyone.* And if I play my role right, I see no reason why I should. I've known a lot of married men, and I honestly believe most of them could be tempted to climb in a strange bed with very little effort. I think their wives are just as ripe for plucking, but that is another story. Ask a wandering male to explain why and you will get any one of a dozen reasons, probably none of which has much to do with the real reasons. The obvious fact of the matter is that while there may be a dozen and one "reasons" verbalized or unverbalized, they all have a direct line to his head, not his genitals. In other words, it's that old male ego. So much so, I'm absolutely convinced no married man *ever* has an affair for reasons of sex. Not that some guys don't claim it is strictly sexual variety they are after. It's easier than having to admit to trying to patch up a bruised or inadequate ego, but that doesn't make it so.

Embarking on an affair, whether for one night or for months, is a dreadfully exhausting business. A man has to spend both time and money on something which is seldom going to prove worth while. Affairs take an awful toll on the nervous system. Sneaking around, trying to keep two women satisfied and quiet, worrying about that masculine image. It's too big a price to pay just for sex. That isn't a put-down of sex. It's just that if it were strictly a matter of demanding glands, I'm sure the guy would make do with masturbation and avoid all the fuss.

I also reject that tired old notion of men being natural tomcats, at least the suggestion that they have a compulsion to prowl any more than women do. That Don Juan complex the psychologists talk about to describe a man who races from one conquest to the next is not a normal component of the personality of Mr. Average Husband. Such a man may try to see himself as stud of the year, but we all know he's merely trying to prove something to himself. And he never quite makes it. The guy who has his masculinity all together knows what he has to offer a woman. He doesn't feel he has to run around collecting equally insecure women to reassure him. Just one *total* woman is enough. More than enough.

To restate the point I made before, however, sex may become boring. If there isn't much variety to it, it *will* turn into a bore. And how do any of us try to relieve boredom? Sure, we start looking for a change. And if a man doesn't start thinking of a change when he gets bored with the gal in his bed, he no longer has an interest in sex. Maybe his inhibitions or his inertia will keep him from acting on his impulses, but don't think he isn't thinking of it. And given that third martini and a waitress with pneumatic boobs and *Look Out!* The boredom, however, is not inevitable. Dr. David Reuben, the shrink who brought us everything we never thought to ask about sex and could care less, holds firmly to that overworked marital numerology which says certain years are more adultery prone than others. For Reuben, the first danger point is during the first year. So much for the honeymoon year! He contends that at that time romance gets buried in a mountain of responsibilities. The guy who hasn't grown up and can't adjust to being a full-time spouse, sticking to one woman, providing for her, and all the rest, will start looking around to start all over with another gal. (Reuben doesn't say why, if responsibility is such a drag to him, he would want to do the thing over again.) The next high-risk phase comes about five years after the wedding. That's when the "newness" has worn off and the husband begins wondering if something else may not offer more. Then last, the man turns middle-aged, and something happens. At age forty-five, he starts fearing his "life is over" and he dashes out to prove to himself it ain't necessarily so. Of course, this is the Reuben system of adultery numerology. Others say the danger years are three years, seven years, age forty years or thirty-five. Take your pick. If you read them all, you can feel secure any year. Or, if you are inclined toward insecurity, you can panic each year. I'm one gal who doesn't choose either. I've watched bed-hopping by both sexes of all ages, and married from five days to over fifty years. It is not a matter of years; it's a matter of opportunity and inclination. And if sex on the home stand gets to be ho-hum, it just becomes a matter of opportunity knocking.

Any intelligent woman, who takes seriously the study and practice of man-pleasuring, can keep a man (and herself) totally satisfied—period. And no, I'm not going to qualify that statement with a lot of exceptions to permit those gals who only half try to get off the hook for accepting the responsibility when their men stray. That world out there is just filled with men who are starved for the loving only a real woman can provide. They wander around like little boys with their noses pressed against the candy store window just waiting to be invited into some sexy gal's bed. And when they do accept the invitation, the housewives back home have no one to blame but themselves, even if they will seldom admit it. I recently talked with a gal who claimed there was nothing she could have done to prevent the affair her husband was having with a twenty-one-year-old divorcée. "What can I do?" she asked in a little-girl whine, not expecting or desiring an answer. "I'm almost forty, my breasts sag, and I have stretch marks from having *his* children. How can I compete with a sexy little thing young enough to be his daughter?" What I could have answered if I hadn't chickened out would have filled the air for an hour. With what she offered a man, she couldn't have held her own with a sensual sixty-year-old. First of all, she looked like a sack of wet putty. At least forty pounds overweight, she seemed bent on doing everything possible to make herself look as if she had just been dragged from a lake bottom after a week's submersion. Makeup, hair, dress. Everything about her came out as sexy as a bunion pad. She said she didn't see any reason to get all fixed up just to stay at home, but I couldn't think of a single reason why a man would want to take her anywhere else. Besides, I do most of my love-making at home. What better place to look my sexiest. If I wore a lot of my "at home" outfits on the street, I'd be arrested.

This self-pitying example of domestic frumpery was also one of the dullest females I've met in many a moon. She admitted she knew nothing about her husband's interests, or his job, or current events. She didn't know what he liked to eat, only what she felt he, and the children, should eat, prepared with a remarkable lack of imagination. And to top it all, she had a list of things she didn't like to do, and would seldom agree to do, in bed with her man. The fact that he would still on occasion approach her for sex seems to me a testimony to some powerful male glands!

Do you remember the story of Scheherazade? As I recall the tale, this Indian potentate had a nasty habit of spending just one night with a gal from his harem then disposing of her like Kleenex the next morning. Scheherazade, figuring she was too young to leave this world, thought up a way to beat the fate when her night came. She started telling the old boy a story which got him hooked like the old Saturday afternoon movie thrillers used to do with kids. It was "to be continued" but always the following night. And she kept this up for 1,001 nights. At least that's the popular, approved version of the tale. Personally, I like to think she had something new to offer the prince in the bedroom that kept him coming back night after night always wondering what new delight she would have to offer. Seems to me it's kind of an allegory, a tale with a moral to it: If you want to keep your man free of any thoughts of straying, just make sure he wakes up each morning with two thoughts: Wow! Last night was fantastic! I wonder what she will dream up for tonight?

I don't mean every night has to be a roll in the hay. The idea is appealing, but most men are simply not up to performing at that rate. But there are many, many ways to pleasure a man in addition to sex, and if a woman is continually adding to her repertoire of man-pleasuring techniques, designed especially for her man, why would he look elsewhere?

The fact is he probably won't unless he's pushed into it. But look out! There are many women careless enough, crazy enough, or stupid enough to dangle other women in front of their men.

Don't ask me why, the real reason, I mean. All I know is that most of these gals would never admit to it in a decade of affairs. No, when their men have a go with some little filly off the home grounds, they go into a proper feminine rage: "Just like all men —all sonsabitches!" And that won't change even on his fifteenth affair with the fiftieth predatory female *she* introduces him to. I don't know whether Dr. Kinsey ever took a poll on the matter, but from my informal research I will save everyone from looking up the results in case he did: A high percentage of men who have affairs are introduced to the "other woman" by their wives. Put your man in a cage with a hungry lioness and don't be shocked if she chews him up.

There is no such thing as an unpossessive woman. Any woman who is not possessive where her man is concerned is either not a genuine woman or she has given up interest in her man and is looking to possess another. Jealousy is not very chic these days. The swingers, jet setters, and bored-but-beautiful people consider it terribly straight and plebeian. But they are the same ones who carp endlessly about feelings of alienation, a lack of meaningful relationships, and the other sensitivity-group jargon which says they have never had anything great going with a loving mate. Show me a sensuous woman and I'll show you a gal who can get decidedly green-eyed and bare-clawed where her man is concerned. And show me an authentic man and I'll show you a man who will tolerate no other male stepping over the boundary of his territory—and he keeps his woman right smack in the center of his territory. Just recently, I was sitting with my man in the night club of a cruise ship. We were talking with the cruise athletic director, a handsome tall blond with a great sense of humor. After a time, our friend asked me to dance. I didn't want to offend him, and I hope I was able to decline in a way which didn't hurt his feelings, but I don't dance with any men other than the one I sleep with. And I only sleep with one man. Would my man have gone into a rage of insane jealousy if I had joined the athletic director on the dance floor? Of course not. That isn't the point. I have two reasons for not dancing with other men. First and most obvious: There is only one man I want to be with, on or off the dance floor. It happens to be my preference, my choice. If the O'Neils and others want their *Open Marriage* and think what I have with my man is "too confining, too oppressive," so be it. I'm hooked on one love affair, and I'm greedy enough to say I've never gotten too much of it. The other reason goes along with it. I don't care for the idea of some perfumed little babe pushing her boobs against his chest on the dance floor. I've heard scores of people say there is nothing sexual about dancing. Well, maybe for them there isn't, but when I have my arms around a man on a dance floor or elsewhere, I know it's a man I'm holding. I haven't danced with a girl since the eighth grade, and I didn't find any kicks in it then. And I'm very sure my man is aware of his manhood when he holds a woman. If he weren't, he wouldn't interest me. So my word to any other females is "Stay clear! I have sharp claws!"

Does possessiveness on the part of a female turn a man off or give him that much talked about "trapped" feeling? Not the sort of possessiveness I'm talking about. Sure, if the gal is a neurotic who goes into a tirade of accusations whenever he is five minutes late coming home, the kind of insecure little thing who is sure every man who isn't manacled, including her own, is laying every secretary behind the water cooler at least three times a day. I think there is a difference between being possessive and *clinging.* The possessive woman says, "This is my man. I'll give him all the loving he'll ever want or need, and more than any other gal can provide." The clinging female says, "I'm a poor, scared little girl. If he is out of my sight and not reassuring me every minute, I'm afraid I'll fall apart." I don't know of any man who wouldn't go bananas with a clinging female wrapped around his neck like an albatross. Besides, frightened little girls make lousy bed partners.

Of course if you want to keep him strictly and exclusively your man, you'd better not only be everything he could dream of finding in a whole barracksful of horny females, you'd better also check those feminine flirtation games when other men are around. I don't care how cute you think you are, or how much ego patting you get out of collecting passes from passing males, or how much you try to excuse your flirtations by saying you're just "naturally friendly, and it doesn't mean a thing." A man wants to know his woman is his woman, that she only has eyes for him, that she looks at him with stars in her eyes and sees him as a combination god, genius, and Adonis, and that she looks at all other men as "no competition" to her man. And if he is that kind of god, genius, Adonis, etc., why in the name of everything that constitutes good sense would any woman want to look at another man—even sideways. And if he isn't, why would she pick him in the first place, or stay with him in the second?

Given a choice, I'd always prefer to be with my man as strictly a pair. That double-dating, the more the merrier business is fine for the high school prom or maybe a bridge tournament in a home for the aged, but for a man and woman who dig a love affair, the groupie thing offers less than nothing. Those dumb parties where the hostess tries to split us up the minute we walk through the door are not for me. If I want to spend the evening chewing canapés with some other woman's man, I don't think it says much good about what is happening between us. And if my man wants others around when we go out, what's happening? Am I that boring? Probably. He likes watching the reaction of other men when I walk into the room on his arm wearing a dress slashed down three inches below discretion. He is secure enough to get that satisfied tomcat look that says, "Eat your heart out, fellas; she's mine." And I'm going to continue to do my damnedest to keep him feeling that way. If I stay strictly on his arm, I know he'll stay in my bed.

A strictly exclusive relationship is definitely not IN today. Nobody lives in an ivory tower, do they? Keep it a twosome and the boring broads up and down your block will be sure you've scrambled your brain. "But don't you feel everyone needs outside stimulation?" they'll ask. It isn't hard to understand what they're saying. Take a look at them. Most of them haven't been stimulated inside or outside for years. Neither have their men. For me, I'll take an exciting ivory tower any day. And I'll serve notice on friends, relatives, neighbors, and coworkers: I'm OFF LIMITS, reserved strictly for MY MAN. As for other women: I'll provide more than his head, heart, and hormones can ever desire. And I keep my claws filed razor-sharp.

A Checklist for You—By Him

Any and every man is seduceible by a woman who uses her head. Well, O.K., maybe not every man. I'll make an exception for homosexuals and those with strange hangups. Let's just say every *normal* man. And any man who can be seduced can be transformed into a superman lover. If he is already your man, and especially if he has put a ring on your finger, you have a starting advantage: You don't have to take him away from any other gal. All you have to do is turn your frog into a lusty Prince Charming, and work to keep him that way.

If you have read this far, you know all the reasons—if you were not aware of them from the start—a woman has for choosing a lover over a husband, companion, father, or dependent little Momma's boy. And the reasons all add up to one thing. Lovers are a lot more fun. And frogs aren't any kicks at all. Which is why I, for one, am such a nut on playing red chips. Whatever can be said of red-chip playing, it represents the ultimate in feminine self-interest.

Two questions crop up when I talk with members of our sex about chip playing. Predictably, many ask, "How can I be sure of the pay-off you talk about? What if a woman keeps giving and giving and never gets anything from her man in return?" To which I answer, "I've never seen it happen." Sure, I've listened to gals tell me of how they have turned it on for a day or two, maybe even a whole week, then when they didn't get him to turn handsprings in response, turned it off. Which obviously is not the way chips are played. The other question is equally predictable. "How can I play red chips and meet his needs and desires, if I don't know what he wants?" The answer is, "You can't." If a guy gives his woman a mink coat, is it a loving act? It depends. What if she is allergic to mink! Or needs and wants a refrigerator more? If I say, "I do want to meet his needs and desires," but I make few attempts to know and understand him and what he really wants from me, I am deceiving myself.

That's common enough, but why? There might be several reasons, but I can think of only two, and maybe they are actually one and the same. Either I don't give a damn about what he needs or wants, or I am afraid to find out. And of course the answer to why I might fear finding out is pretty obvious, isn't it? If I ask him, I am at least implying I am willing to give it. What if I am Little Miss Uptight, and I ask my man what he would like in sex, and he comes up with a long-held dream of doing some wild, wonderful things with body oil while watching a porno movie under a mirrored ceiling? Sure! I jump on my psychological bike and backpedal like mad. If I ask my man what he might like for dinner, I'd better be willing and able to turn out something better than a tuna casserole.

Hard-core, visceral-level honesty is not something most of us seek with a passion. We run after our men pleading, "Tell me you love me," but almost never, "Tell me what you want changed in me." Like the Wicked Witch gazing into her mirror, asking, "Mirror, mirror on the wall, who is the fairest of them all?", we only want to hear flattering things. If we are drab in the kitchen, dumpy in figure, dull in conversation, and dismal in bed, we don't want to hear it. Well maybe we should. If we don't, we just might find out too late.

And now for a way to find out just where you stand with that man of yours and what you can do about it. But, of course, there is a catch and here it is. Are you willing to take a few hard

lumps? And maybe get some valuable information in the bar-
gain? O.K. Take the following checklist to your man. Ask
him to check, with brutal honesty, the attributes in a mistress—
physical, emotional, intellectual, and sexual—which turn him on.
Then ask him to go back over the list, with even more candor,
checking those which he sees in you.

If you expect him to be frank, you can't play games. Let him
get the idea you are only asking for a snow job, and you will
push your female hostility into third gear if he sees you as anything less than sex goddess of the decade, you will snow no one
but yourself. Take your lumps. There isn't a one of us who
could hope to score 100 per cent. We can each, however, employ the information. We can get to work on ourselves.

And don't, whatever you do, argue about how he checks you
out. I may see myself as the most everything gal who ever
joined a man between the sheets and over the morning coffee,
but so what? If he sees me as a bushel of dried mushrooms,
what good does my opinion do me (unless I can find a gorgeous
man who digs a gal who looks like a bushel of dried mushrooms)?

A further don't: Don't tell yourself it—whatever IT is—can't
be changed. Just about anything about us can be changed. What
with diets, exercise, silicone, and surgery, I can even do just
about anything I set out to do with my figure except grow three
inches. So take a firm grip on your ego and hand him a sharp
pencil.

Her Physical Self

HER OVER-ALL FIGURE

	HER	WHAT TURNS YOU ON

Slim
Voluptuous
Pleasingly plump
Angular
Proportioned
Squat
Top heavy
Bottom heavy
Adolescent
Matronly
Dumpy
Tall
Topless dancer
Boyish
Clothes model
Muscular
Fat
Skinny
Sexy
I never really noticed

HER BUST

	HER	WHAT TURNS YOU ON

Firm
Flabby
Upthrust
Small
Medium
Large
Huge
Pointed
Pendulous
Bouncy
Siliconed
Saggy
Ripe
Two fried eggs
Just like dear old Mom's
I never get a chance to see them

HER HIPS

HER   WHAT TURNS
YOU ON

Pattable
Broad
Slim
Plump
Bony
Voluptuous
Teen-age
Straight
Frozen
Lumpy
Sexy
Matronly
Fluid
Boyish
Firm
Inviting
Flabby
A sack of potatoes
Great!—for a running back

HER CALVES AND ANKLES

	HER	WHAT TURNS YOU ON

Fat
Tapered
Skinny
Smooth
Hairy
Stubbly
Bony
Flabby
Straight
Sexy
Athletic
Boyish
I wouldn't know; I'm not a leg man

HER THIGHS

HER   WHAT TURNS
YOU ON

Stout—and then some
String bean
Matronly
Straight up and down
Flabby
Sexy
Bumpy
Boyish
Firm
Touchable
Tapered
Built for hot pants
Strange, but not bad
Firm
Smooth
Why do they make me think of weight-lifting?

HER HAIR

	HER	WHAT TURNS YOU ON

Inviting
Stringy
Dull
Prim
Flowing
Cute
Girlish
Matronly
Untouchable
Plain
Lustrous
Elaborate
Bushy
Unwashed
Tinted
Sensual
Lacquered
Neglected
Clipped
Excessive
Just right for a pillow
Bald—in a sexy way

HER MAKEUP

	HER	WHAT TURNS YOU ON

Painted
Sparse
Casual
Theatrical
Prim
Natural
Conservative
Sexy
Messy
Youthful
Matronly
Bizarre
Enhancing
A women's libber
Virginal
A Playboy bunny
A hooker—at the end of a workday

Her Emotional Self

	HER	WHAT TURNS YOU ON

Introspective
Pouty
Childish
Petulant
Placid
Cheerful
Hysterical
Explosive
Long-suffering
Peevish
Accepting
Castrating
Understanding
Controlled
Hostile—is a copy of her mother
Warm
Unpredictable
Frigid
Moody
Bland
Tearful
Rational
Sarcastic
Defensive
Strictly sexual
Saintly
Insecure
Calm
I'm not sure; she may be dead

Her Intellectual Self

	HER	WHAT TURNS YOU ON

Well informed
Shallow
Well read
Insightful
Deep thinking
Poorly informed
Turned on by her man's interests
Broad interests
Intellectually motivated
Stimulating conversationalist
Mostly woman talk
Opinionated
Narrow
Anti-intellectual
Intellectually curious
Intellectually snobbish
Cultured
Boorish
Stimulating
Challenging
Insecure
Smug
Stupid
Complex
Pleasingly dumb
Pseudointellectual
A woman intellectual? You're kidding!
Just smart enough to pleasure me

Her Sexual Self

	HER	WHAT TURNS YOU ON

Eager
Curious
Reserved
Cold
Passionate
Aggressive
Demanding
Athletic
Passive
Free
Rigid
Seductive
Experienced
Manipulative
Vain
Insecure
Confident
Experimental
Argumentative
Fun-loving
Likes erotic bathing
Resentful
Shy
Great with massage
Puritanical
Submissive
Loves nudity
Exhibitionistic
Strange

HER   WHAT TURNS
YOU ON

Digs variety in positions
Oral sex
Mutual masturbation
Active
Superior lay
Rejecting
Inhibited
Wild
Naïve
Sophisticated
Anal sex
Lesbian leanings
Perpetually horny
Bored
Soothing
Ladylike
Castrating
Critical
Non-committal
Childish
Initiates sex
Enjoys sharing fantasies
Turned-on by a vibrator
Unpredictable
Maternal
Insatiable
Thinks it's only for making babies
Goes for erotic movies, books, etc.
Loves my body
Kinky
Totally dead—and I'm looking around